THE COMPLETE
IT RECRUITMENT
SURVIVAL GUIDE

THE COMPLETE
IT RECRUITMENT
SURVIVAL GUIDE

The Definitive Handbook for
IT Recruitment Consultants,
Resourcers and HR Professionals

AYUB SHAIKH

Holistica IT Training Publications
London, UK
www.holistica.co.uk

Distributed by Troubador Publishing Ltd and Holistica Consulting Ltd, UK

ISBN 978-0955636-301

A CIP Catalogue In Print record for this book can be obtained from the British Library

Acknowledgements

I would like to show my appreciation to a whole host of people who were instrumental in bringing me to this juncture in my life. Many were key figures who knowingly or unknowingly aided in imparting knowledge and shaping the experiences that form the core of this book. Others were simply there as a constant source of cheer and support in the background. I can't assign hierarchy since they have all played their roles with total and unwavering commitment. Not least, my sincere thanks go out to all of my past mentors and managers in the IT, recruitment and training industries who have propelled me to this point. I have been blessed by a steady stream of individuals throughout my life who have never held back from offering the right advice and showing me the opportunities that lay ahead. You all know who you are and this book is as much an accolade to you.

To my wife Naureen, I am eternally grateful. Throughout life's ups and downs you have always been there as the backdrop to my life. Quietly and serenely providing endless love, and support which a mad dreamer and adventurer like myself simply takes for granted most of the time. You remind me whenever I look at you of all that is truly important in life, and your mere presence soothes away all of the commotion that my outlandish schemes bring into our life.

To all of the training managers, directors and CEOs from Holistica's regular client base, I say a heart-felt thank you. You have done me the honour of allowing me to take on that huge responsibility of training up your staff. Without your faith in me Holistica would never have progressed within this industry, and I would not have had the platform from which to write this book. You are to me the giants in my life and I salute you all.

To all of the attendees on my courses, this book is as much the story of you as it is of me. I offer my total gratitude to you all for your encouragement and enthusiasm whenever we meet. Thousands of delegates from a myriad of backgrounds, and I feel honoured to have been there when you took your first few steps into the world of IT recruitment. I can only count myself as being incredibly fortunate to have earned your respect and friendship. You are the inspiration for this book.

To all those who urged me on when I first set up Holistica and also pushed me during the production of this book, I say a huge thank you. Specifically to my dear friends Imtiyaz Hajat and Sayeed Shaikh and to my brothers Altaf Shaikh and Rizwan Shaikh. All of whom, not only with this book but generally in life, seem to always be there to get involved with steering me through the trickier situations, I thank you. Thank you also to Dr. Rehana Seedat for her advice when reviewing the chapters, and to my dear friends Ghulam Rezbi, Kafeel Abbas and Dr. Aleem Mirza for always being there at the other end of the phone with sincere professional advice or simply words of encouragement. Between training events when I was in hotels, and airport lounges around the world writing chapters and trying to meet deadlines you were the ones I turned to, and I want you to know that I appreciate it.

I'd also like to offer many thanks to Jeremy Thompson at Troubador Publishing Ltd for his continuous effort and attention in compiling this work, and to the proof readers and typesetters who got involved in this mammoth task. Also my thanks to Randy Glasbergen for drawing such perfect cartoons and to Naeem Mahmood for his help in the designing the book cover and for constructing a cracking web site.

And finally, to my mother Khadija Shaikh and my father, the late Yusuf Shaikh. He unexpectedly passed away before the book could go to press, and yet it was he who more than anybody else on the planet eagerly awaited the final product to proudly show off to his friends. For as long as I can remember you both have always done whatever you could to clear the path so that I might push ahead with my own goals. I thank you for both for always being my staunchest advocates and an inspiration in my life.

Contents

Introduction

And so it begins!

Whether you are an IT recruitment consultant, a CV resourcer, or the person tasked with that all-important IT HR function for your company, I hold out my hand and welcome you to this industry. You're in for one hell of an adventure.

In this industry you'll meet a diverse range of people, both young and old. Some of them will be simply awe-inspiring characters, astounding you with their depth of IT knowledge and experience. Trust me, you'll only come to fully appreciate *their* talents once you have absorbed some of the material in this book and began to realise what they are truly all about. Others who come to you will be less impressive, 'fledgling techies' just starting out in IT with you at the centre of their world; their guiding light. But, if you stick around long enough within IT recruitment, you'll eventually experience the satisfaction that comes with seeing those same raw recruits develop into established decision makers who themselves come back and hire from you. There will be failed interviews, as well as pleasant surprises. People who you thought were a 'cert' to get the job will fail miserably, and those who didn't apparently stand a chance will make it all the way through to the end. Be it helpdesk analysts or Technical Architects you will be placing individuals into positions that are pivotal to making the business world move forward.

As you move through the chapters of this book you'll undoubtedly sense the sincere respect and utter passion I have for some of the innovative concepts that were borne of IT, and for some of the major characters that spawned these ideas. I make no apologies for any of this. After all these people communicate with inert molecules of Silicon and make them sing the song of life. There is no other industry like this. IT impacts every aspect of the world we live in. It pulses through the fibre of our lives, continually evolving and astounding us. Enhancing the way we communicate with each other, dictating how we record our music, and even guiding us effortlessly on our car journeys. IT allows us to capture images using mobile phones no bigger than credit cards, and enables us to store thousands of those images on storage media no bigger than a child's finger nail, or simply compress the entire photo album and whizz it across to our relatives on the other side of the planet in the time it took you to read this sentence. Once you absorb the material in this humble offering, I guess I secretly want you to ultimately feel the same passion I do when you return to your work. If you find yourself recounting any of these stories to your partner over a meal in a restaurant well outside your hours of work, then my job is done!

Why this book?

Firstly let me say, *I know your pain*. I am guessing that since you have taken the time to seek out this book in particular, you already find yourself (as with thousands of others in your field), trying to sound credible in front of IT bods who seem to communicate in a totally different language. You are surrounded by IT job specs that are seemingly written in some sort of alien syntax, and you then find yourself trying to match these enigmatic job titles to jargon-filled CVs that are nothing more than page after page of technical acronyms which make absolutely no sense to you. And when you attempt to seek clarification from any of the IT experts you meet, their explanations leave you even more baffled and in greater need of Aspirin than when you started. Fear not, for help is at hand. You're simply in need of an easy-to-read map, and a willing guide. Someone who can explain the IT industry and IT concepts to you in clear light-hearted terms; and describe the IT roles and the jargon to you in ways that make sense. I have always been proud to be considered a mentor for the thousands of IT recruiters I meet around the world every year during my training events, but now I consider it a particular honour to be chosen as your helping hand and your guide through the seemingly complex terrain that is IT recruitment.

About the Author

You have to be a rare (and slightly strange) tri-part being to really enjoy writing a book like this. Firstly, you need to have an unhealthy passion for all things IT. Secondly you must sincerely enjoy imparting this knowledge to those from a sales/business/recruitment background, knowing that they aren't necessarily as geek-ish as yourself. And thirdly you need to have had firsthand experience yourself of working in an IT recruitment or HR environment so that you know how much IT knowledge is just enough in order to come across as confident and credible when it matters. This is the path that I have had the great fortune of travelling. Not necessarily out of design but certainly out of love for all three areas.

The Student: I graduated from Kingston University with an Honours degree in Aeronautical/Mechanical Engineering in the early nineties. What was apparent to me upon my departure from the hallowed halls of Kingston, was that I certainly didn't want to spend the rest of my life in a wind tunnel shaving bits off a wooden mock-up of a wing section, or indeed sitting at the control panel of a nuclear power plant in the Hebrides. What had really caught my imagination in the final year of the degree though was the IT aspect of the course.

The technophile: During the degree we were learning to program in an old engineering-oriented language called Fortran, and making robotic arms dance around to the lyrics of our machine code. This, to me, seemed like a far more exciting industry to be in. Between lectures we had started to play with CAD (Computer Aided Design) to help us design components. In our spare time my friends and I had started to experiment with exciting new software on a new device called a PC with a radical new interface called Windows, and were even sharing files with people across the world using this screechy new thing called a modem. Even the media was awash with tales about the phenomenal success of characters like Bill Gates and Larry Ellison. Naturally upon graduation I would never get down and dirty with an aircraft engine ever again.

The IT trainer: My first real job after graduation was as a trainer for a small IT project in the City of London. I was starting to really learn about applications and operating systems and even how to set up networks. And I was then getting paid to impart that knowledge to larger and larger groups of people. I loved it. Eventually I moved over to a much larger operation set up by one of the ex-directors of Learning Tree, the then largest IT training company in the world. The new business was to be called Informator and we were providing technical systems training to blue chip organisations ranging from Merrill Lynch to British Airways. I eventually became UK Manager of Informator. It was at this time that a CEO of an IT recruitment company in London had seen me give a presentation and subsequently made me an offer I couldn't refuse, to start up a new division at his fledgling company CitiElite.

The IT Recruiter: I immediately had an affinity with IT recruitment. It allowed me to develop sales and business development skills whilst remaining within the IT industry for which I had such a huge passion. My IT recruitment career reached its zenith a number of years later at Robert Walters plc in London. As a seasoned recruiter I also found myself mentoring and training up new recruits as they joined the team, not only teaching them the sales and recruitment aspects of the job but also clarifying the IT terminology seen on CVs and job specs. This also reminded me how much I loved training.

The Industry Trainer: Around the year 2000 it was time to somehow bring all three aspects of my career together, and in this year I founded Holistica

Consulting as the first company in the UK (or indeed the world as far as we know) to provide a range of courses purely geared towards teaching IT and telecoms recruiters everything they need to know in terms of being more credible and confident when dealing with people from the business. Eight years on and I am fortunate enough to find myself having trained thousands of new and established recruitment consultants, resourcers and HR specialists from many of the largest recruitment companies around the world. I am called upon to give coaching sessions and to advise division managers and CEOs. Today Holistica's training is on the induction programme of numerous IT recruitment companies, as well as a key element on the staff development programmes of blue chips companies such as ING Bank for their own HR staff.

How to use the book

Hopefully you will soon find out that this is a guide like no other. Not a reference manual but an enjoyable reading experience full of anecdotes, historical perspective, fascinating stories, and even (dare I say) humour. In this handbook I will share with you all of the knowledge and insight I have picked up as a seasoned IT recruiter and an IT recruitment trainer over the last eighteen years. I am also aware that you won't always have the time or luxury of reading each chapter as a full narrative, you'll want to jump straight in to the key bits of information that count prior to a meeting or an interview. For this reason I have created at the beginning of each chapter a 'Straight to' grid to enable you to quickly leap frog to the key areas.

As well as this, most of the chapters relating directly to IT roles have been structured so that you can quickly jump to

- The role in detail
- Key responsibilities of this role
- What we should see on their CVs
- Key skills and characteristics
- Interviewing tips for this role
- Summary sheet for this chapter

I sincerely hope that you enjoy using this book on an ongoing basis and that it does indeed become the companion to your career.

This is the world of IT recruitment. I hope that The Guide will encourage you to jump in and explore!

PART

A BRIEF HISTORY OF IT FOR RECRUITERS

CHAPTER ONE

The Evolution of IT

Introduction

Trust me, I know. I know how daunting it can seem to dive into IT recruitment for the first time. I've seen it on the faces of colleagues when I worked in the industry. The trepidation when you initially start to browse through IT CVs and technical job descriptions; when the world starts to look like a very unfamiliar and complex place indeed. However, if you currently find yourself in this position, let me allay your fears a little. For there exist key snippets of supplementary knowledge that are pure gold. They can be quickly acquired, and when learned, will prove to be invaluable in accelerating your progress towards becoming that credible and confident recruiter in IT.

GLASBERGEN

"I don't understand #11...
Thou shalt not be obscene
on the Internet."

Once Upon A Time ...

Around 1.5 million years ago a group of primates, known as *Homo habilis*, split off from the rest of their Australopithecine cousins. A tiny yet significant occurrence within one of their family groups would became the pivotal act that would go on to shape their destiny. This species would become *Homo erectus*, *Homo sapien*, and eventually go on to become the dominant force on the planet. This tiny act was the use of a sharp-edged stone flake to kill and butcher a large beast, and then to use the same implement to tear open the thick, furry skin. Something which was previously impossible with the teeth and fingers which nature had issued them with. They had just invented the Swiss-army knife of their day! There and then a particular axiom had became indelibly etched into the minds of all future generations of the human species. That, when the going gets tough, your chances of survival are directly proportional to the quality of the *tools* you can unleash on the situation.

Around 1.5 million years later, another group of human beings around the world realised that the rules of survival in business were about to be blown away by a new way of thinking. Rather than in the caves of their forefathers, this new breed worked behind the scenes in the science laboratories and garden sheds across the land. They would launch a new and innovative concept that would eventually change everything – Information Technology. Companies which refused to grasp the concept or embrace the tools which were borne of IT, would quickly be assigned to the group labelled '*corporate extinctus mortificus*'! Those who '*got it*' quickly realised that IT could be used to automate many tasks, take care of the finance and accounting functions and dramatically reduce the time it took to bring products to market. Ultimately computing could enhance profitability for those who chose to adopt it, and would leave behind those who ignored it. This was to be the dawn of IT, the birth of the IT department, and therefore the birth of the IT recruitment industry.

Not Just a History Lesson

This chapter contains one of those foundation snippets of wisdom, to help start you on the journey towards achieving that ethereal aura of experience and wisdom in IT recruitment. If you're involved in hiring IT experts at any level, it is imperative that you firstly understand how the gradual changes within the IT industry affected the formation of the IT department and the IT roles which you currently deal with.

The evolution of the IT department is as an important topic in itself and is discussed in more detail in the next chapter of this book – for now I'd like us to absorb some fundamental concepts. Moreover, I would strongly suggest that you don't attempt to tackle the next chapter without first becoming fully acquainted with the historical timeline of how computers themselves evolved into the corporate environment. Not only will this give you a historical perspective on this industry but also, when speaking to senior developers, technical architects and project managers, it will give you an air of having a far more seasoned persona. And, trust me, that always go down well!

So that is what this chapter is about. Don't think of it as a simple history lesson – but as a primer outlining the major events in one of the most exciting industries on the planet today. Your industry. And, yes, if you're looking to bolster your IT vocabulary, and increase your fluency in *techno-babble*, then this process also begins here. This chapter will begin to explain many of the terms and concepts that you will see on job descriptions and CVs.

This timeline or historical description of how computers evolved is well documented in IT, and is generally referred to as the **Five Generations of Computers.** It's also a very easy way to appreciate how companies arrived (in an IT infrastructure sense) at where they are today. As you delve deeper into other chapters in the book, you'll also realise that you need some of this foundation knowledge in order to understand most of the IT roles properly.

So without further ado, let's look at this Five Generation timeline.

The Five Generations of Computers

The First Generation (circa 1940–1955)

Or "What's that buzzing sound?"

I think it's probably safe to say that you won't be seeing computers from this era on your current job specs or CVs, but nevertheless, we need to show due respect and reverence for these clunky old machines which were the forerunners of all IT as we know it.

Figure 1.1
An early vacuum tube as used in the ENIAC.

'First Generation' computers started showing up around the early 1940s to the mid 1950s and they all displayed key physical characteristics. These were devices that used big, temperamental **vacuum tubes** at the heart of their circuitry, and stored their data on magnetic drums. They were big. Really big! If what you're visualizing at this moment is a contraption out of Dr. Frankenstein's lab from the original black and white RKO movies, you've gone too far back – *but only just*. These enormous devices could fill an entire warehouse, and needed a great deal of electricity to keep them alive.

At the heart of their workings were the many rows of vacuum tubes that would diligently chatter away in their binary conversations (not sure about 'binary'? Don't worry we'll grapple with that later).

Indeed the first of these machines, the Mark 1 and the ENIAC (more on these devices later also) often caused blackouts in surrounding areas due to their voracious thirst for electricity.

These early computers also emitted a tremendous amount of heat which often meant that, whenever the giant air conditioners in the room broke down, insects (generally moths) would quickly build nests and set up home in the warm innards of these machines. So when it came to finding and fixing the many problems that arose in those first computers, engineers could often be heard muttering under their breath
"Oh no! It's more of those damn bugs in the system."

And so the term 'bug' stayed with us to imply a problem or fault within IT.

Communicating with the First Generation Computers

These early machines weren't clever enough to understand complex commands or communicate in any method approaching 'human conversation'. They couldn't understand basic English language structure or even single word commands. Their logical circuits were far too primitive at this stage.

First Generation Languages: Binary

The 'brains' of these early machines were based around the concept of switches and relays. Their processing circuits comprised a myriad of switches (in the form of vacuum tubes shown in figure 1.1). And since switches only have two states; **on** or **off**, these states could be thought of as **zero** and **one**. We needed a mathematical notation or language which could somehow represent any number using just two states.

Without going into any great detail on the way this mathematical language works, suffice it to say that **binary** was the method through which early programmers would communicate directly with these switches. They would communicate directly with the very 'core' elements of the computer. Binary language is a weird and abstract concept, which actually dates back to 800 BC, and a mathematician in India. It is a mathematical system which comprises only two numbers, zero and one; and allows the user to represent *any number* you can think of using just those zeros and ones.

At this point you're either developing a mild headache or a cynical smirk around the corners of your mouth. No problem, I sense both of these in the response of the audiences whenever we get to this section of a training course. Whenever I'm teaching this topic it's always amazing to see the looks on the delegates' faces as they slowly grasp this bizarre new way of thinking. As they slowly realise that in the world of binary, any number you can think of can indeed be represented with just a group of ones and zeros.

I'm not going to go mad here in trying to teach you the rudiments of binary. But I can leave you with what is often left on the flip chart at the point when most

Binary Ref Numbers						
64	32	16	8	4	2	1
1 = 1 in binary						1
2 = (1x2) + 0 = 10 in binary					1	0
3 = (1x2) + (1x1) = 11 in binary					1	1
5 = 101 in binary				1	0	1
14 = 1110 in binary			1	1	1	0

of my students in class experience the 'Ahhaaaah – I see it!' moment.

(See above.) Get it? Yes... no? Possibly?

For the readers who haven't quite grasped it, don't worry, binary is in no way an obligatory skill in order to speak with developers today. *Thankfully we've left those days way behind us.*

If you think you do understand binary, then the following witticism (shared with me by a candidate one lunchtime) will make sense. If you happen to find it amusing, be afraid... because it really isn't that funny! It actually means that you are slowly coming over to the *geek side* of the force (and you should be advised that eBay is currently doing a very good line in anoraks).

GEEK HUMOUR
There are only 10 types of people in this world. Those who understand binary and those who don't.

Using binary early programmers would converse directly with these machines using punch cards or ticker tapes in this simple coding technique. The hole in a punch card meant one, and the lack of a hole stood for zero.

Important Point: This programming directly onto the heart of a computer

"No, I don't remember which button I pushed."

is still referred to today as **low-level programming** because one is speaking directly to the chip. These were the early days of programming, and the luxury of being able to communicate with computers using English type commands, such as **if** and **goto**, would only arrive much later on with the advent of **high-level languages** (see page 225).

Let's now take a quick look at some of the computers from the first generation.

Computers from the First Generation

In 1941 the Mark I was created by Harvard University and is often thought to be the first electrical computer. It used electromechanical relays to verbalise the 'on/off' mathematics of binary. But in real terms the Mark I was very quickly trounced by ENIAC (Electronic Numerical Integrator and Computer) the 1946 brainchild of boffins from the University of Pennsylvania.

The ENIAC is widely considered to be the first digital computer.

These early machines were huge, the ENIAC used 17,500 vacuum tubes, covered 1800 square feet and weighed 30 tonnes ... and yet its processing power could easily be out-matched today by a low-end PDA, mobile phone or play station.

Figure 1.2
The ENIAC. This early photo doesn't show its entire 100ft length.

The vacuum tubes were notoriously unreliable, each one lasting around two days before it burned out. In fact five days of smooth running, without any blown tubes, was a very good working week indeed! A little known fact was that most of the early programmers of the ENIAC were women, all of whom were later acclaimed as being amongst the first female pioneers of computing.

There followed a plethora of early machines, each one displaying more powerful

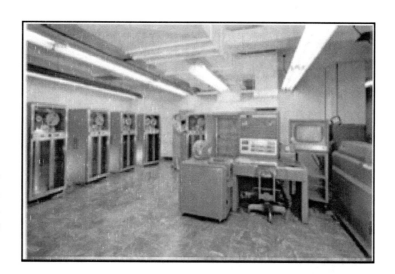

Figure 1.3
An IBM 704 mainframe (image courtesy of LLNL).

processing than its predecessor. Notables from this list of Golden Oldies include **UNIVAC** (Universal Automatic Computer) and the **Cray** series of machines.

1mm square of a modern silicon chip has more processing capacity than the entire ENIAC computer.

The list of first generation computers also includes:

*   Zuse Z3
*   Colossus
*   Atanasoff-Berry
*   BINAC
*   EDSAC
*   SEAC

'Massive', 'over-priced' and somewhat 'senseless' were commercial descriptions that stuck with these early machines. But this was all about to change. A significant invention in the area of electronics was about to prove itself to be the catalyst for rapid evolution to the next phase of computing.

"Computers in the future may weigh no more than 1.5 tons."

A quote from *Popular Mechanics* 1949 in an article making predictions about the future of technology.

Second Generation Computers (circa 1955 to 1965)

*or **The Transistor Revolution***

Around the late 1950s a device know as the transistor began to replace the old cumbersome vacuum tubes as the building blocks of their circuits. And the world would change dramatically. A transistor was an amazing thing indeed. Amazing and yet very efficient to manufacture. This was an incredibly cheap and reliable way of manipulating tiny electrical signals in a computer's circuit. It was yet another inspired creation from that hotbed of early IT creativity, **Bell Laboratories** (we'll come across Bell Labs again throughout the book and especially in the chapter on Operating Systems).

Size Does Matter

A small transistor could replace up to 40 vacuum tubes and gave off virtually no heat. It is fairly safe to say that without the creation of transistors and their associated digital circuits we wouldn't have been able to experience the frenetic progress and increased miniaturization that marked the following years of the computer industry.

Figure 1.4
A range of transistors old and new. Did you spot the current day version at the far right?

Miniaturization of the circuits meant that second generation computers therefore also started to come down in size (though don't be tempted to think of anything approaching 'desktop' or even 'bedroom wardrobe' sized machines just yet).

The term '**mainframe**' started to be used to describe this new generation of computers. These stylish mainframe machines weren't small by today's standards but they certainly didn't weigh the 30 tonnes of the old UNIVAC machines. You also didn't need to allocate an IKEA-sized bunker to house your new corporate workhorse. The term '**midrange**' also came about to describe some of the smaller sized machines.

Second Generation Languages – The Dawn of Assembler and High-Level Programming

Staying with second generation computers, things were changing in terms of programming too, and developers of the day were starting to question their approach. Surely, they thought, there was a slicker way of actually communicating with these new devices. It was generally agreed that binary (also known as **machine-code** programming) was a laborious pain. So around this time programmers were starting to formulate a new generation of language called the **assembly** (or **assembler**) languages.

Assembler languages became a *translation layer* between the binary-based thinking of the computer and the English-based thinking of the human! This meant that for the first time programmers didn't have to speak to the computer in it's own machine code. They could now actually use *English type* commands such as ADD, IF, GOTO and PRINT. And a translator called an 'assembler' or '**compiler**' would then take care of the messy business of converting all of the English syntax into binary for the machine. Programmers would no longer have to get their hands dirty dealing with all those low-level zeros and ones.

This idea of **higher-level programming** would take hold and *not let go!* The programming fraternity would never look back. Indeed, with the advent of compilers, future generations of programmers would be able to spend far more time focusing on the actual creation of exciting new business applications without having to worry about the dreaded conversion back to binary.

More critically, programmers around this time were starting to demonstrate how useful their skills could prove within a commercial business environment. The new programs being created were demonstrating how IT could potentially help businesses improve efficiency and therefore increase profitability.

Commercial organisations were starting to take notice, and pay a great deal more interest to these 'new-fangled computer things'. And all of this meant that the *funding* was on its way!

Third Generation Computers (circa 1965 to 1970)

or IC! I see!

Unsurprisingly, the focus on size was to continue relentlessly. Transistor miniaturization became the rage in the mid-sixties, and these components eventually became so small that hundreds, even thousands were eventually placed onto a single wafer of silicon chip to form the world's first **integrated circuit (IC).** Those computers, which had ICs at the heart of their operations, were commonly referred to as **Third Generation computers**. Companies such as IBM and Digital made key landmark decisions to base their company's entire future strategy on producing world-changing machines like the **IBM System 360**, a name designed to imply that IT hardware could now become involved across all 360 degrees of the business spectrum.

Third Generation Languages

Programming languages were also continuing their own quiet revolution. New and more powerful **third generation languages** (3GLs) such as **C**, **Cobol** and **Fortran** were becoming increasingly divorced from the binary of the old days, and were developed much more around the needs of the programmer. So third generation computers were starting to be programmed via a keyboard and screens. These **'higher-level'** third generation languages meant that there wasn't a binary-speaking punch card in sight!

Enter the Modern Mainframe

Far from being a noisy, cumbersome eyesore, the mainframes of the third generation started to look almost majestic. Sitting in their purpose built de-humidified surroundings, some resembled thick black glass pillars, whilst others stood as imposing white monoliths with their sleek gleaming glass cabinets and arrays of glimmering lights.

Around the mid-seventies modern mainframes also started to enter popular culture and were beginning to capture the imagination of the movie going public. They were now being iconocised by sci-fi films of the day such as Arthur C Clarke's *2001 – A Space Odyssey*, which centred around a gleaming black mainframe named **HAL** (named cryptically after the letters of IBM – can you spot the link?).

HAL constantly questioned its creator as a small child might do (yes, it spoke). And upon being instructed to shut down for the greater good of the project, it whispered the immortal line '*Will I dream?*' For the first time not just mere processing but the concepts of intelligence, creativity and even emotion were being associated with these mechanical devices – albeit in films. Hereafter, IT and Hollywood would become entwined in an enduring love affair.

By the early eighties mainframes would become *the* essential item for any self-respecting corporation. These third generation machines were now truly powerful yet very expensive devices. The cost of joining this privileged IT club, typically hundreds of thousands (even millions) of dollars, would automatically preclude small-to-medium sized businesses from joining. Moreover, the entry price would guarantee that the 'Fraternity of Corporate IT Users' would for some years remain an exclusive club. The beneficiaries of this new technology would be limited to a highbrow clique consisting of large investment banks, universities and government departments.

Figure 1.5
An IBM zSeries z800
Type 2066, using
Linux.

And so the trend continued apace. In the early eighties the computer industry was continuing to boast more and more impressive performance figures, being able to carry out certain basic calculations in a billionth of a second – unthinkable previously. Computers were in the news and in the movies. Suddenly this 'new' industry was starting to capture the imagination of the world. And now a fun pastime amongst industry gurus was that of predicting how far and how fast this progress would continue.

Enter one of the pioneers of integrated circuitry, **Gordon Moore**, the co-founder of Intel.

Moore's Law

Observing the rate at which computers were changing, i.e. getting increasingly smaller in size yet correspondingly more powerful with it; Gordon Moore put forward a rule of thumb which is well known amongst the IT industry as Moore's Law.

Moore's Law effectively states that

> "The processing power of an IC (Integrated Circuit) will approximately double every year."

The law has been modified of late i.e. that the processing power nowadays doubles approximately every eighteen months instead of twelve months. Even so it's fairly safe to assume that the computer you buy for yourself this Christmas will generally be either half the size or twice as powerful as its predecessor of last year.

Moore of course was absolutely right. The pace of change in IT was impressive indeed. But it was still all about to get a lot more interesting!

Let's enter the Fourth Generation.

Fourth Generation Computers (circa 1970 to present)

or *Let's get Personal!*

If Integrated Circuits were cool in comparison to early transistors, the 'microprocessor' was about to take the game to a totally new level.

With the advent of the Intel 4004 chip in November 1971, the world for the first time saw how it was possible to incorporate the equivalent processing power of an entire room full of first generation computer hardware onto a single silicon chip no larger than a digestive tea biscuit. The public psyche was being readied for a huge breakthrough in IT.

Previously unimaginable was the idea of *personal processing power*; computing for the average man and woman on the street. After all, it was only a few years previously when IT was the domain of the elite (and the *corporate* elite at that). But the time of *consumer computing* was upon us. The world was about to witness the advent of the world's first **Personal Computers**.

The First Personal Computers

It was IBM who ventured into this market with their first portable entry-level device with the catchy little name of the **'IBM 5100'**. It cost a mere $10,000 to the end buyer and, by IBM's own later admission, didn't really perform too impressively even as a first attempt!

However in 1981 IBM created their first PC aimed at the consumer. The operating system (**MS-DOS**) for this machine was contracted out to a young programmer called Bill Gates who had just started off in IT with his fledgling company, Microsoft.

At around the same time another company **Apple**, headed up by Steve Jobs, was busy readying the launch of a their own personal computing architecture. And, in 1984, Apple launched **The Lisa.** This became one of the one of the first commercially available PCs to use a **Graphical User Interface (GUI)**, and was a forerunner to the mighty **Macintosh**.

Apple launched the Mac PC in January 1984, in a now famous advert called '1984'. This ad was aired during a Super Bowl interval, and was directed by none other than Ridley Scott (of *Alien, Gladiator* and *Blade Runner* fame). The depiction was in line with George Orwell's novel showing a young female runner brandishing a hammer with a view to smashing down the rule of 'Big Brother' (an unsubtle hint at the ongoing reign of 'IBM'). The strap line at the end read

"Get an Apple Mac – and 1984 won't be '1984'."

The Court Cases Begin

"It's like we both had a rich neighbour (called Xerox) and you say 'Hey that's not fair you stole his TV– I wanted to steal his TV first!'"

That's a paraphrase of the famous retort from Bill Gates to Steve Jobs after the court case in which Microsoft was accused of stealing the GUI design concept from Apple. Gates was referring to a Xerox device known as the '**Alto**' which most IT analysts still consider to be the world's first GUI-based PC, and which Steve Jobs had initially seen on a site visit to Xerox in 1979.

Apple and Microsoft had subsequently both been heavily 'influenced' by this concept as a design for their own operating systems, and the following legal battle ended the idea of a single company owning exclusive rights to the GUI concept. The resulting competition within the industry of course left us, the consumer, with fourth generation computers which even today are evolving at a tremendous rate in terms of power and application.

However even the most passionate PC addicts amongst us have still not experienced computers which we could truly class as 'Fifth Generation Computers'.

The best is, as they say, yet to come. You won't find these devices under your Christmas tree in the immediate future, but that shouldn't stop us discussing the whole idea of ...

Fifth Generation Computers

or *The Dawn of Artificial Intelligence*

Computers and robots which are able to think for themselves. Devices which can so closely emulate the human thought process, that they can be thought of as 'intelligent' or even 'creative.' These aren't mere flights of fancy or descriptions of scenes from the latest Will Smith science fiction movie, but the realm of Fifth Generation Computing (and their associated Fifth Generation programming languages). In short, this is the area of **Artificial Intelligence (AI)**.

An interesting titbit about AI as an example of life imitating art. The whole concept of AI and robotics was made popular by the science fiction writer Isaac Asimov, long before the scientific community were ever involved in these areas. Asimov (author of *I, Robot*) actually created the terms 'robot' and 'robotics' for his fictional novels, but thereafter these terms began to be used by programmers and scientists to describe Artificially Intelligent man-made objects — and entered common usage.

Pioneers in AI

Japan is amongst the leaders in this area and has been chasing the dream of a single epoch-making intelligent supercomputer that would make the PCs of today seem like the vacuum tube oldies of yesterday in comparison. After considerable time, effort and money being ploughed into projects such as the **Fifth Generation Computer Systems project** (FGCS) in Japan, the idea of creating such mega-computers seems to have abated.

However, organisations such as Honda continue with a dogged determination in this area. Originally just a novel four-foot tall humanoid device which could walk and stand on it's own, **ASIMO** (named after none other than Isaac Asimov, mentioned above — but also standing for **Advanced Step in Innovative Mobility**) has now evolved into a very impressive example of AI robotics.

You might recognise the little fellow below. He (if it is a 'he') has recently starred in the Honda television ads in the UK, but there are also a number of good clips on the Honda web site to show how far this project has come. ASIMO now has speech recognition capability, can run around corners and even dance! His human-like movement and intelligence is disconcerting, his dancing is simply scary.

Figure 1.6
ASIMO from Honda.
No modern home
should be without
one.

Checkmate!

In 1997 the world of AI was pushed centre stage once more when an IBM supercomputer called **Deep Blue** (note how IBM's new products often have 'blue' in their title – IBM's nickname in the industry is **'Big Blue'**) took on and beat the reigning world champion Kasparov in a six game chess tournament. Reporters then asked a very disgruntled Kasparov if he thought that Deep Blue did truly use AI or just sheer overwhelming processing power and logic. The grandmaster confirmed that it had to be AI. When asked how he could be so sure, Kasparov revealed that during one of the games he actually initiated a complex trap deep within his gaming strategy to see if the computer simply followed set routines as most chess computers did. What he realised as he headed towards defeat was that Deep Blue had suspected the trap well ahead of time and re-engineered its own strategy in order to triumph.

Summary

So there it is. That was a simple introduction to the evolution of IT, and more specifically the Five Generations of Computers. Armed with this knowledge you can now forge ahead towards understanding how the IT department had to change with each new generation.

And that's where we're going in the next section of this book. We're going to get even closer to the individuals who you'll be recruiting and working with! Let's look now at the Evolution of the IT department.

The Five Generations of Computers

First Generation

- Communicating directly to the CPU using zeros and ones
- Also known as 'low-level programming' or machine code
- Associated with the ancient computing technologies
- Each program was created with a particular machine in mind

Second Generation

- Assembly (or 'assembler') language
- One step away from machine code so needs a translator (or 'assembler') to convert what we've written back into machine code

Third Generation

- Higher-level languages than Assembler
- Easier for humans to understand
- Use English-type commands such as **Let**, **goto** and **if**.

Fourth Generation

- Higher-level than third generation therefore even less complex coding required from the programmer to achieve results
- Closer to the natural human language structure
- Includes querying languages and visual data presentation languages

Fifth Generation

- Artificial Intelligence

CHAPTER TWO

The Evolving IT Department

Introduction

As someone involved in IT recruitment, without doubt, you need to become familiar with the whole idea of how the IT department came about and the major events which shaped the IT department of today. In fact, the story of the IT department is really a case study in adaptation to change, and is inextricably linked to the five generations of computers discussed in the last chapter. However, not even the most astute IT analyst could have foreseen the twists and turns that would shape the IT department as technology meandered forward from those unsteady first steps.

STRAIGHT TO

➢ Evolution of IT recruitment
Page 24

➢ Mainframe linked to dumb terminals
Page 28

➢ Smart terminals
Page 29

➢ Understanding client-server architecture
Page 33

➢ Understanding thin clients
Page 35

"My mom has the coolest job in the world.
She's a director of human racehorses!"

The Evolution of IT Recruitment

From an invisible entity in the very early days of mainframes and dumb terminals, through an era of networked PCs, and on to an age of networked mobile devices, the IT department has evolved, changed in size, shape and indeed its sphere of influence. In the 21st century you simply can't have a business model without IT. Indeed in the first decade of the 21st century we're already starting to experience the next heady wave of leading edge hardware, software and communication technologies; and one can only assume that the IT department is yet again on the verge of another metamorphosis. So, let's take a look at how the IT department changed in line with the five generations of computing.

The First Generation IT Department

Or *"Noisy but good"*

There wasn't much of an IT department to speak of during this first generation of computers, essentially because there weren't really any users to look after! Most of the early machines were clunky old contraptions predominantly used for scientific and research purposes, and the people who were interested in using the computer's processing power were invariably the same individuals who were living side by side with the machine, entering the data and re-programming it as required. If things went wrong, they too were the only ones qualified to fix any problems that arose.

So in these early years, think of the IT department as less of a department and more a group of very inconspicuous and softly spoken individuals who would tend to gather at their own table in the corner of the staff canteen away from everybody else. They had been seen at one time or another wandering around in the corridors but nobody really knew what they did. After lunch they seemed to disappear into one of the large unmarked rooms somewhere in the bowels of the building. They were too introverted to be management, and seemed to be too officious looking to be the building's plumbing engineers.

The IT department as we currently know it would only really take shape as the second generation of computers began to arrive on the scene, along with a very pragmatic business user.

The Second Generation IT Department

The second generation of computing was really the era when *true* business computing took off, and this of course meant the rise of the business user. These were users who for the first time had not the slightest interest in *how* this new technology worked; just that it worked and stayed working. They wanted results, quickly and effectively. A small band of IT experts was therefore initially assigned to care for this new IT infrastructure, and to be around for users when they might face problems.

It was no longer going to be just sympathetic IT literate technophiles who would now be tapping into the mainframe; but demanding and pragmatic business users could potentially draw on its capabilities too. The mainframe would now be directly influencing the trade floor for the first time. Though physically sited in its original central location, it now reached out to the desks via a nervous system of copper cables, and each user was given a desktop device of their own to complete the link. This was the era when the IT department was group of people supporting…

Figure 2.1
The DEC VT-100. One of the early dumb terminal type devices.

Mainframes linked to Dumb Terminals

In this first networked business architecture for business users they were given '**dumb terminals**' to enable them to tap into the processing power of the mighty mainframe. These devices were called 'dumb' for a reason. Unlike modern PC's they had no internal processing power and therefore were totally incapable of 'thinking' for themselves.

Dumb terminals were manufactured without hard-drives so

they had no storage capability of their own. At this time processing and data storage were both extremely expensive, and certainly not going to be wasted on the likes of the average user on the trade-floor. Dumb terminals were simply 'portals' which allowed the user a look into the mind of the mainframe, displaying relevant data via the '**green screen**' (a term which also became a euphemism for the dumb terminal). GUIs (Graphical User Interfaces) hadn't been invented yet, so there was no mouse and therefore no user-friendly icons to allow the user to navigate around. When the dumb terminal was switched on, the user was greeted with nothing more than a single blinking cursor on an eerily barren green landscape; an apt metaphor for the all-seeing mainframe which was effectively saying

"Go ahead – punk! Type something... I dare you!"

These were the days of the **Command Line Interface (CLI)**.

A simple keyboard allowed the user to initiate the link with the mainframe and input data directly into the mainframe's storage banks. If truth be told, the majority of 'business users' in this era of computing were simply glorified data entry clerks. And this layout suited the IT department perfectly.

The IT department loved this era, and here are the reasons why:

- They were revered as the first generation of techno-wizards! Nobody outside of the IT department could really comprehend how these ethereal beings managed to commune with the mainframe. This new breed of human could somehow communicate with that huge computing brain at the heart of the corporation, overseeing a device that was so quickly becoming a predominant part of everyones' working life. The mystique that surrounded this new department started to take seed at this time. The 'geek' was born. When things went wrong with your dumb terminal, or the data wasn't flowing properly, you would have to pick up the phone to one of these wizards and explain your problem. They would listen intently and knowingly, and the line would then abruptly go dead. As a user you could then do nothing else but stare slowly upwards towards the ceiling as if trying to peer into another dimension, only to imagine what manner of sorcery was at work up there beyond the hidden veil of the third floor. Twenty minutes later the battle was over and the magicians had tamed the beast once more. The dumb terminals flickered back to life once again obediently.

- This 'dumb terminal to mainframe' set-up is also referred to as a **centralised network**. This means that the only device in the network that was really 'thinking,' or processing, was the host mainframe. Strictly speaking this 'centralised architecture' also meant that each dumb terminal was hard-wired directly into the mainframe (and not via a hub or router) and relied on this central processing power to look after everything. Importantly, this meant that the whole network could be administered from a central location.

- Anything that went wrong nearly always occurred at the mainframe end because this is where the 'brains' of the network were. This didn't matter because the IT department spent most of their time tending this machine and guarding it as much as possible against downtime.

- Dumb terminals were such simple low-maintenance devices (no floppy drives or input methods other then a keyboard) that users couldn't introduce problems into the network. In the first generation of dumb terminals there was simply no way to introduce your data other than through a keyboard. However this would soon change with the advent of 'smart terminals' (which were the more powerful cousins of the dumb terminals and which came with some processing) and later on with the introduction of the PC.

- This neat and easily controllable configuration meant that risk of virus attack was low and there was always a high level of security.

There's a Quick Glance Summary sheet overleaf to remind you of the story so far.

IT department in the
Mainframe - Dumb Terminal Era

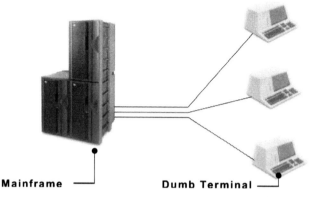

Mainframe

Had all the processing power and controlled the network.

Dumb Terminal

Had no processing capability. No floppy or hard drive. Useless without the mainframe.

ADVANTAGES	DISADVANTAGES
▪ Centralised network means total control over users. ▪ Single point of maintenance. ▪ Users have no power other than what's given to them. ▪ Scalable. As users increase just keep adding more dumb terminals.	▪ Slow for the users. ▪ High cost of mainframe excludes all but the largest corporations. ▪ No Graphical User Interface. ▪ When the mainframe stopped working so did everything else.

The Third Generation IT department

or "Now that's a Smart Machine!"

As mainframe technology moved forward into the 1970s (now harnessing the newly discovered power of integrated circuits) the user terminals also started to evolve. In some organisations dumb terminals were starting to be replaced by their more sophisticated cousins. A **Smart Terminal** was one endowed with a modicum of computing power. It often had enough processing capability to offer a graphical display of sorts (though nowhere near the true GUI capabilities of the future devices). However, even with the greater take-up of IT in business, during this third generation many organisations decided to stay with dumb terminals at the user end. Therefore the IT department didn't really need to change the way it worked at this time.

But there were those in the IT department who could sense that something was very wrong. They knew that very soon they might have to work a lot harder. For looming on the horizon was a new type of architecture which IT boffins were beginning to discuss earnestly around the world. There were rumours of a **desktop architecture.** This small device could operate entirely on its own, even without a network if need be. This new **Personal Computer** was akin to a single-user mini-mainframe, with its own built-in hard drive and far more processing power than any smart terminal could offer. There was nothing wrong with that in itself, but many organisations were thinking of bringing these into the workplace. And that was simply asking for trouble.

Many in the IT fraternity could sense that this new age device was about to give the networked user their own power. *Too much power.* And, in so doing, would present the IT department with a whole new range of problems.

We were about to enter the fourth metamorphosis for the IT department.

Fourth Generation IT Department

The Advent of the Corporate PC and the Fat Client

The coming of the **Personal Computer** was inevitable. Many companies were starting to jostle for position in an attempt to dominate this market. IBM and Apple became two key companies who would throw down their gauntlets first (see page 17).

Although this was a device designed to allow the small business and home user to embrace the brave new world of IT, many large organisations also decided to replace their decaying dumb terminals with these new powerful personal computers. Company Directors were rushing in where experienced techies feared to tread. In fact, IT Managers around the world were blissfully unaware of the user-led chaos that would soon engulf their operation.

Why the IT department loathe PCs

PCs at the users' desks were proving to be a nightmare in terms of IT support. Suddenly all the control and order associated with the previous dumb terminal era would vanish in a puff of GUI-driven hysteria.

By the late eighties and early nineties the PC revolution had hit the streets with a vengeance. PC retailers had started to appear in every shopping precinct, and this item became the one commodity which no home could do without. This new enthusiasm and transformation in the public persona manifested itself differently at work, and not in a nice way. The old maxim of 'a little knowledge being a dangerous thing' never rang more true.

The IT department soon started to flounder, as suddenly

- Everyone wanted to come into work. Not to *actually* work, but because the PC at work was far more powerful than the cheaper one at home. And

- There was a floppy drive or (if you were really lucky) a CD ROM. You could load up your own software at will. All of those important little domestic chores could be looked into during work time.

- All of the PC games ran a lot better on the more powerful work machine. And, of course, it was also a great way of trying out that dodgy piece of pirated software you purchased at a boot market over the weekend.

- Managers couldn't tell if you were really working or upping your score on Tomb Raider. PCs always made the user look good whatever you did *as long as you peered seriously and intently at the screen.*

- Private data could be stored on your own personal hard drive away from the prying eyes of the company's IT department.

- For those who were more unscrupulous, it was an opportunity to transfer data over to their own hard drive to be extracted later and viewed at their leisure.

Figure 2.2
Why IT departments loathe PCs.

- As a result of all of the above viruses became rife. They spread frequently and mercilessly, attacking the very IT core of companies. And in the early days we didn't have a clue. There was no protection at all against the new enemy!

All in all, networked PC's or '**Fat Clients**' rapidly became the bane of the IT department. To this day they remain a source of much downtime and failure in any organisation which has not implemented the necessary restrictions and security precautions.

Understanding Client-Server Architecture

At this juncture we need to explain the term **'Client-server'** as it is a term which you're undoubtedly going to see on CVs. Most of your networking candidates will refer to the network they have worked in as being some variation of a client-server architecture. So let's explain this now.

Around the 1980s we all stopped referring to the network as being comprised of the 'big machine upstairs linked to the less powerful user machines on our desks'. Instead the IT community laid down the following definitions:

A Server: Any machine (though in a large organisation this would invariably be a mainframe) that acted as the central processing device to which the (less powerful) user machines were attached in a network. This device also housed the database and any of the centralised applications which were going to be needed by the user.

A Client: Any device (which, by definition will always be less powerful than the server) that is networked to the server, and which relies on the server for much of its applications and data. A client can be fat or thin; and this is dictated by how much processing and storage the client has. So a PC with its own hard drive and lots of processing power is a very fat client (also referrred to as 'thick' client).

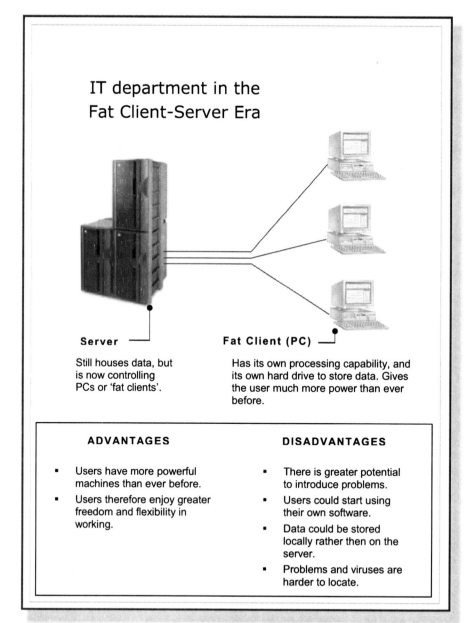

IT department in the Fat Client-Server Era

Server ───

Still houses data, but is now controlling PCs or 'fat clients'.

Fat Client (PC) ──

Has its own processing capability, and its own hard drive to store data. Gives the user much more power than ever before.

ADVANTAGES	DISADVANTAGES
▪ Users have more powerful machines than ever before.	▪ There is greater potential to introduce problems.
▪ Users therefore enjoy greater freedom and flexibility in working.	▪ Users could start using their own software.
	▪ Data could be stored locally rather then on the server.
	▪ Problems and viruses are harder to locate.

The Dawn of Thin Client-Server Architecture

or "Let's Take Back Control!"

By the late 1990s IT departments were so fed up with the continued onslaught brought about by networked PCs or 'fat clients' that they themselves pushed forward a network revolution which would bring back control and tame the unruly user once and for all.

Techies had secretly hankered for the good old days – the days when they were perceived as wizards. The days when the mainframe was the only thinking machine, networks were easy to control and the user knew their place. In other words, the days of the dumb terminal. The problem was of course, that users would never go back to that Orwellian scene again. They would no longer go without their powerful machines, their GUI interfaces and their Internet access. So any change would need to be executed with stealth. Almost invisibly, and so cunningly that the user wouldn't notice a major difference. The IT industry came up with a concept of the **thin client** (also referred to as the **NC** or **Network Computer)**. In essence, what they re-introduced was a dumb terminal for the 21st century.

This move has proved so successful that most large data-rich organisations have already adopted a **thin client-server** network. Any large organisation that has suffered data theft and virus attack due to a rampant user base, has already implemented *thin* clients. I'm hoping that, having defined fat (thick) client earlier, you can start to work out for yourself how we define a thin client.

Opposite is a summary of the properties of thin clients.

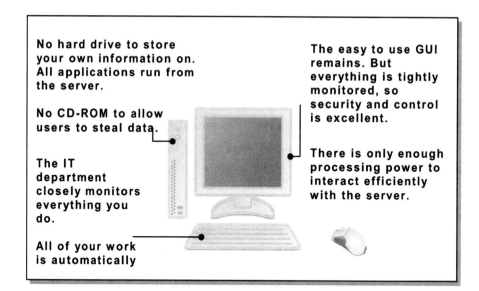

Figure 2.3
The advantage of
Thin Clients (from a
business
perspective).

Thin Client Vendors

Below are listed a number of companies which specialise in thin-client
architecture, many of which may appear on CVs or job specs:

- Citrix
- Wyse Technology
- Neoware Systems
- PXES Universal Linux Thin Client
- Sun Microsystems
- Hewlett Packard

IT department in the Thin Client-Server Era

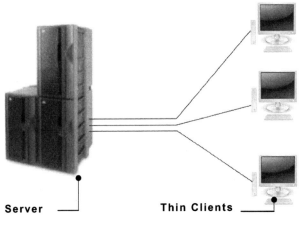

Server ——┘

Power once again returns to the mainframe.

Thin Clients ——┘

Users are once again brought under control. Thin clients are like dumb terminals for the new millennium.

ADVANTAGES	DISADVANTAGES
• Centralised network means total control and protected data.	• Users feel restricted. No more autonomy.
• Return to single point of maintenance.	• When the mainframe stops working, the network comes to a stop. With PCs the users could have continued working in some way but with thin clients there is nothing that can be done.
• Users have no power other than what's given to them.	
• Scalable and cheap. As users increase just keep adding more thin client machines.	

How IT Roles Fit into the IT Department Today

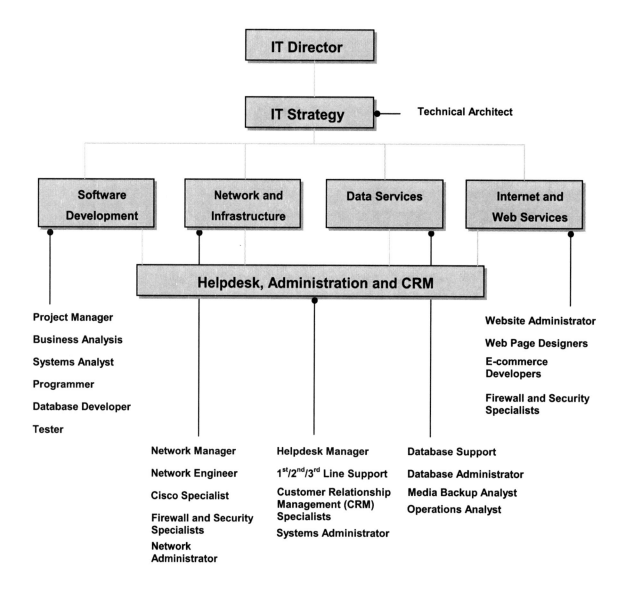

Project Manager

Business Analysis

Systems Analyst

Programmer

Database Developer

Tester

Network Manager

Network Engineer

Cisco Specialist

Firewall and Security Specialists

Network Administrator

Helpdesk Manager

1st/2nd/3rd Line Support

Customer Relationship Management (CRM) Specialists

Systems Administrator

Database Support

Database Administrator

Media Backup Analyst

Operations Analyst

Website Administrator

Web Page Designers

E-commerce Developers

Firewall and Security Specialists

Summary

So that was the evolution of the IT department to the present day. This chapter should have made you realise that the function of the IT department, and therefore IT recruitment is a constantly evolving concept. It has undergone a number of changes over the last forty years, and we are by no means able to predict with certainty which form it might take ten years from today. Wave after wave of new technology concepts continue to pound us as we enter the new millennium, and so it seems there will be no let up in the desire to implement these new systems into the corporate environment; which, let's face it, all points towards a busy future for IT recruiters.

**"It's bad enough I'm bombarded with images
of skinny fashion models and actresses, now
I have to look at a *thin computer* all day!"**

PART

IT Fundamentals
for Recruiters

CHAPTER THREE

A Simple IT Model

Introduction

Now that we have gained a thorough knowledge of the history of IT (from the previous chapters), we now have a stronger footing on which to further explore some key IT principles. Before we start delving into the complexities of each key IT role, it's worth getting to grips with a few fundamental IT concepts in lay terms so as to build that solid foundation; and that's what this chapter is all about. The knowledge you gain here will help you better understand the terms and concepts you'll come across on CVs and job specs. But first, feeling hungry? How about a delicious slice of homemade cake, just like granny used to make!

STRAIGHT TO

➢ Basic computing concepts
Page 45

➢ Categorising hardware
Page 47

➢ Basic software concepts
Page 50

Sweet and Sticky: The IT Layer Cake

At the simplest level we can think of any company's IT system as being constructed somewhat like a three-layered sponge cake!

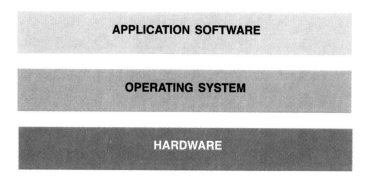

Regardless of whether the IT system in discussion is a single PC, a corporate level IBM mainframe, a Nokia mobile phone, a satellite in orbit around the earth, or the fly-by-wire system controlling the aileron and rudder movements of an Airbus aeroplane – the above three layer model generally holds true.

IT systems (generally) are made up of

*   A topping of Application Software sitting on

*   A central layer of Operating System (OS) which sits on

*   A bed of Hardware

It's almost impossible to be living in the 21st Century (let alone be involved in IT recruitment) and not harbour some misconceptions about many of the above terms. So let's assume for the moment that we really are starting with a clean slate and define everything clearly. The simple concepts introduced in our layer cake analogy are summarized in the diagram on page 45.

Basic Software and Hardware Concepts

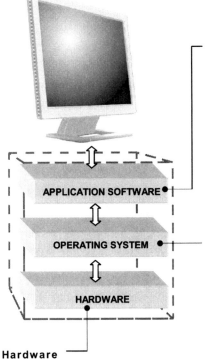

Application Software

All the useful business tools such as word processors, accountancy software and web design packages. Also games and entertainment software. These are presented to the user via 'peripheral' hardware such as keyboard, mouse and monitor (these peripherals are also controlled by the Operating System).

Operating System

Brings the hardware to life and establishes a 'platform' to allow useful application software to run on the hardware. Also enables peripheral devices (mouse, keyboard, monitor) to work.

Hardware

Includes the computer's motherboard, hard-drive, mouse, keyboard and monitor.

Layer 1: Hardware

In a sense this layer of our IT model is the easiest to define.

*   Hardware exists physically – it's not an abstract concept (which some might say of software). PCs, laptops and PDAs are what most people perceive to be 'the IT in their lives'. But of course they are simply referring to the external embodiment of IT. There is a lot more going on underneath the surface.

*   Secondly, IT hardware is all around us and seldom a day goes by where we haven't bumped into a computing device of some sort; be it a PC, laptop, iPod, PDA, mobile phone or even the satellite navigation system in your car. Hardware is all around us.

Hardware, however, is useless on its own and would be but a meaningless collection of dead components without the **operating system** to breath life into it, and control its every heartbeat (chipbeat?). Furthermore, those bottom two layers of IT (hardware and OS) would be no fun at all without the application software which brings about all of the true functionality which we associate with our computers. When we walk into PC World, the shelves are

"I think you'll be impressed with my technical
skills, especially after you realize I'm a hologram."

stacked with a range of intriguing application software pleading with us to take them home and start designing our new landscaped garden, retrace our family history, or drive up to the Lake District using the shortest possible route.

Categorising Hardware

Let's look at some key classes of hardware in more detail by understanding that most IT hardware falls into one of the following categories:

Mainframes

The history of these was outlined earlier in Chapter 1. They are the large and expensive computers which corporations rely on to run their networks. They can support hundreds or even thousands of user machines (clients) on a given network and are the centre of IT focus for most large businesses. The company associated with mainframes from the dawn of modern IT is **International Business Machines (IBM)** though many other organisations also produce mainframe-type hardware.

Supercomputers

These are less talked about in business circles, although they are often more powerful in processing terms than their mainframe counterparts. The reason for this is that, whereas mainframes are the heart of a network of hundreds of business users and can accommodate many users working with many different applications at the same time; supercomputers generally dedicate all of their processing power to a single yet immensely complex task.

A prime example would be the supercomputer used by the British Meteorological Office to forecast global weather patterns. This requires all of the huge processing power of a supercomputer focused solely on an incredibly complex set of mathematical calculations. Other examples are the use of supercomputers to create the ever more impressive animations and special effects (otherwise know as **CGI – Computer Generated Imagery)** seen in Hollywood blockbusters such as in the recent Star Wars trilogy, the Transformers movie, or in any of the Disney-Pixar animations.

Personal Computers (PC)

The emergence of PCs and Macs was discussed in detail in Chapter 2. These are of course the epitome of consumer driven IT devices and the showrooms and shelves of your local PC retailer are testament to the success of this breed of hardware. When used as the end-user device in a network, they are often referred to as **fat** or **thick clients** within a **client-server** architecture. This whole concept is discussed in detail in Chapter 2.

Network Computers

A **Network Computer** or **NC** is again a particular type of **client** machine used within a client-server architecture, and was discussed in detail in Chapter 2 They are also referred to as **thin clients** because they have no hard drive (so the user is unable to store data on their own machine), and have minimal processing (so users can't introduce their own software or customise their own machines). The issuing of NCs was an attempt by businesses in the mid-to-late 1990s to re-capture power for the IT department and restore higher levels of control and discipline over users who had started to run amok with the powerful PCs they were issued with in the early 1990s. In Europe **Citrix** is a company which will appear time and again on the CVs of your candidates who claim to be specialists in 'thin' client server architecture. Citrix specialise in introducing this type of network to your clients, though there are a myriad of companies to choose from if your business decides to go thin. This whole scenario is described as a major transitional episode in the evolution of IT on page 35.

Clusters

Take a situation where data and applications have to be available to all users in a robust and timely manner, without fail. The most effective way of achieving this high availability and security is by setting up two or more servers (often mainframes), or a **cluster**, housing the same data and applications. The group of servers can be connected together and keep each other updated as to the state of things. This enables the workload to be spread and allows ease of administration and maintenance.

Blade Servers

Blade server technology is one which allows the processing power of an entire mainframe server to be housed in a slim self-contained unit (known as a blade enclosure). A single blade enclosure has all of the necessary components relating to power, cooling, storage etc., but all are enclosed in a compact layer of hardware just a few inches thick (with the overall dimensions of say a large attaché case). The neat thing is that blades offer a **modular** approach to increasing your server capacity. This means that as your IT needs increase there is no need to buy an expensive new server, you can simply add additional blades, so that ultimately you end up with a large cabinet full of compacts 'slices' of server, much like a giant vertical box of technology-flavoured After Eight mints.

Grid Computing

Grid computing is a very neat hardware concept which treats many separate and **heterogeneous** (described on page 162) IT systems as one coordinated pool of potential IT power.

In this way large computational problems can be solved by drawing on all of the disparate systems and focusing their attention on a single challenge. A good example of this is the 'SETI@home' project. **SETI** (Search for Extra Terrestrial Intelligence) is the project to find signs of life in outer space, but even their supercomputer isn't powerful enough to single-handedly analyse all of the data that pours in from around the world's radio telescopes. So they have created a grid computing capability that allows you, the humble user at home, to directly help them in their search, utilising the spare capacity of your home PC. Once you download their software and install it on your PC – it then becomes a part of the grid! Whenever you're away from your PC, i.e. making a cup of tea or on your lunch break, the SETI supercomputer will tap into your PC's idle time. So your humble machine rather then going to sleep and displaying some boring screen-saver, can divert its effort to the very important task of helping find E.T!

The Software Layers

So let's turn our attention to layers 2 and 3; the software layers of our IT cake. Continuing with the theme of simplicity for a bit longer, here's some more good news; there are really only **two** big categories of software which you need be concerned about. *Just two.* Sounds easy enough I'm sure you'll agree. These are:

• Operating Systems (Systems Software)

• Application Software

However, you might want to hold on tightly to that feeling of lucidity for a minute, *as I'm pretty sure you might need it later on.* Nothing in IT is that simple. It probably won't surprise you to learn that these two classes of software can also be broken down into further sub-categories.

With that in mind, let's wade out a little further and explore these facets of software in more detail.

Layer 2: Operating Systems

Operating systems can be separated into two important groupings. Operating systems fall into those:

• From the Unix family (and which are said to be 'open') and

• Those which are non-Unix (and said to be proprietary or 'closed')

To understand this whole area of operating systems we require a complete section of the book, and so this concept is covered in much more detail in Chapters 4, 5 and 6.

Layer 3: Application Software

Similarly, application software can also be broken down into further classes of software which generally fall into

* Off-the-shelf (OTS) software

* Enterprise Resource Planning software

* Middleware

And these distinctions also need to be understood fully if we are to converse with programmers with any level of confidence. This is a huge topic to which we'll dedicate an entire section of the book. Chapters 13 to 19 are all about **Software Development**.

Summary

For some of you it may be have been an insultingly simple chapter (in which case, not to worry, the limbering up session is almost over), as we have the juicy stuff on its way). For the rest of you, your first few teetering steps towards IT recruitment fluency are over, maybe it's time to get your water wings on, and paddle out a bit further into the deep end. Make no mistake about, 'The Guide' from this point onwards starts grappling with the real issues of IT recruitment. Acronyms and concepts are going to start flying around thick and fast. But no need to worry, as ever, we will keep it light-hearted and fun.

After all, 'The Guide' is forever patient, forever understanding!

Let's take a closer look at operating systems.

GEEK HUMOUR

Two rather nerdy programming students were walking across campus when one said, "Where did you get such a great bike?"

The second student replied, "Well, I was walking along yesterday minding my own business when a beautiful woman rode up on this bike. She threw the bike to the ground, took off all her clothes and said, 'Take what you want.'"

The first programmer nodded approvingly, "Good choice. *The clothes probably wouldn't have fit.*"

CHAPTER FOUR

The Importance of Operating Systems

Introduction

Have you ever noticed how, in the Hollywood blockbusters, there are never any issues relating to IT compatibility? The baddies from some sinister underground terrorist cell can always immediately open up the applications and read the data which they found on the 'heavily encrypted' optical micro CD stolen from the CIA around ten minutes earlier. Soon after that Tom Cruise can pop that same CD into a device built into the heel of his shoe, and hey presto! It all works. Not only does it work, but with an interactive 3D graphics capability that makes the best PS3 games seem primitive in comparison!

STRAIGHT TO

➢ The purpose of an OS
Page 54

➢ The key functions of an OS
Page 58

➢ Categorising operating systems
Page 60

➢ Summary sheet
Page 61

"My dad is a natural at multitasking. He can goof up, screw up, and mess up all at the same time."

Even aliens from a million light years away can somehow fire-up and read any email we send them. In fact in *Independence Day*, Jeff Goldblum simply had to create a quick virus on his Apple laptop, and upload it to the alien mother ship to trigger a failure in their entire IT system, catastrophic enough to bring down the whole fleet. *The whole fleet!* How did our intrepid hero know they weren't running on a Microsoft OS or, that having come half way around the galaxy, they hadn't had the foresight to install a half-decent firewall?

Meanwhile Back on Planet Earth

The reality for us of course somewhat different. Operating systems **(OS)** are actually the backbone of IT. We choose operating systems based on our long-term needs; the hardware we prefer and the applications we wish to use. But once we have made our choice, we have then committed to work in a certain way. Applications which are designed for one proprietary OS will generally not work on any other OS (though this is now changing). If using a wide variety of Off-The-Shelf (**OTS**) software is important to you and you don't foresee yourself having to develop bespoke software, then a Microsoft OS might be appropriate. If however, other issues are important such as future-proofing your IT investment and creation of lots of complex bespoke applications, then you might decide on a Unix OS. Either way this whole are of choosing and committing to a particular operating systems is an intricate equation which needs to be solved at the highest level.

The Purpose Of Operating Systems

Operating systems have one overriding purpose in life. Simply to *'bring your computer system to life'* and to keep that system functioning properly! So although operating systems don't really *appear* to doing anything **useful** they work tremendously hard behind the scenes. As mentioned in the previous chapter, operating systems are also referred to as **systems software** and of course include software such as Microsoft Windows and Linux. However, you can't write a letter with just Windows XP on your computer, or touch up your holiday snaps with just a Linux OS on your machine. All of the *useful* things which we associate with our computers are often outside of the remit of operating systems and generally fall within the dominion of **application software**.

However it is also important to understand that without operating systems, application software couldn't even be installed onto a piece of hardware. There has to be an operating system to act as the interface between the hardware and all of the useful applications we use. Without an operating system *IT simply doesn't* work!

The astronomic wealth of companies like Microsoft are built on the back of single world-changing operating systems such as the ubiquitous Windows, which went on to become an operating system legend. One that would for decades be intrinsically linked to the world's favourite consumer IT architecture, the PC, in a partnership which would eventually come to be known as **WINTEL** (**Win**dows on In**tel**).

An Interesting Analogy

One intriguing analogy to describe the whole concept of operating systems came about *in situ* during a training session in Leeds a few years ago. The recruitment consultancy being trained was a particular favourite of mine, mainly because of the diverse backgrounds from which they seemed to recruit their new consultants. It was always an interesting crowd. On this occasion one particular lady in the audience was a bright young thing who had just graduated in psychology. She offered an interesting cognitive parallel to coincide with what we were discussing.

"So if the human body can be thought of as the complete IT system, our brain must be the operating system."

She offered, and waited with expectation – as did the rest of the audience. I must admit I was momentarily stumped, and had to think about the veracity of what had just been offered. She was definitely on to something – but was it an accurate enough representation to be rubber-stamped as a bona fide analogy? These are the times when trainers are forced to make such strategic decisions. Say 'yes' and get on with the schedule of the day, and hope that no one will take it any further. Or, think it through and see if something interesting can be weaned from it.

And then it hit me!

"No. Not quite."

I was emphatic in my manner, but I had to be. I was pretty sure I could take the idea she was running with, but it just needed some fine-tuning.

"The human body is the hardware. The brain is the CPU (in fact the chip and motherboard), and it consists of two types of software – conscious and sub-conscious thinking."

The audience stared back through narrowed eyes which highlighted their mild cynicism at what was to come.

"Wait… indulge me for a minute…" I continued.

"The sub-conscious part of the brain can be thought of as our operating system. It regenerates our bones, grows our hair, controls our organs, regulates the pumping of our blood (seamlessly and automatically even while we sleep), it fights off infections, and keeps everything ticking over nicely without our intervention…"

They were still listening.

"The conscious part of our brain on the other hand, is that which contains our habits and skills, is the 'application software' of our lives! That is the stuff we've picked up from the people around us, learned from our education system, or absorbed form the environment in which we grew up. This is the stuff that allows us to do the 'useful' stuff such as speak different languages, cook Thai green chicken curry, drive cars and write love letters. The operating system for us humans remains the same – because nature doesn't push out as many new versions as Microsoft – but our application software (the learned stuff) keeps changing as we progress in our lives!"

They were stunned. The bemusement on their faces dissolved and was replaced by 'Ahaaa's!' and knowing smiles.

It's an analogy I still use today.

The Wizard of OS

It's no secret that a software house can become quite wealthy on the back of a successful idea for a new application software. It happens every day. But if a company manages to introduce a revolutionary new *operating system* to the world, one that gets accepted as the OS to a mainstream device worldwide; then that company ceases to be just another ordinary software house. From that point it sets itself apart from the rest of the herd, and becomes a market-changing paradigm. The stuff of IT folklore.

In most encyclopaedias of IT if you attempt to look up the phrase 'market-changing paradigm' or the 'the stuff of IT folklore', the entries will usually read *"See 'Microsoft'"*. Which is why we dedicate a summary sheet to this family at the end of Chapter 6.

So firstly lets clarify. What specifically do operating systems do, and why are they so important?

The Key Functions of An Operating System

The key functions of any major operating system include

*   Ensuring that the BIOS (Basic Input Output System) is working when you power up your PC. This means that the chip at the heart of your computer becomes ready to communicate with the on-board devices and the application software you have installed.

*   Ensuring that all the correct device drivers are present. This is needed so that the OS can take control of peripheral devices (such as your mouse, monitor, keyboard etc.).

*   Controlling the processor (chip) and monitoring its status. The OS monitors all of the ongoing processes at the chip level and ensures that your computer's silicon heart isn't over-worked.

- Laying down a system for organising files and data on the hard drive. This is known as the disk or file support system, and is a method of chopping up and arranging files and data so that it's easier for the OS to organise everything. So for example on your PC you might be running Windows, which typically uses the File Allocation Table system commonly known as FAT 32 or NTFS file system support. If you were running Linux on the other hand, it might prefer to use its own system (examples being ext3 or GFS).

- Providing a GUI (Graphical User Interface). Most modern operating systems come with a GUI front end so that you, the user, can easily interact with the OS and therefore the applications on your computer. It wasn't always this way of course. Older systems used CLI (Command Line Interface) where you simply typed in instructions from the keyboard (otherwise know as the *dark ages* of user interaction).

- Controlling a network of computers. All modern operating systems (certainly the ones you see on candidate's CVs) will be capable of networking to some degree. Many of these will incorporate middleware for handling a myriad of different technologies across a large enterprise network. Middleware is explained in more detail on page 166).

- Maintaining external and internal security. It's the operating system that is configured to monitor the security status of processes that are running on the computer or network. Security threats are perceived by the OS as being external or internal. External security is primarily all about ensuring that users and external programs logging onto the system are restricted in terms of what they can do. For example an OS would know which parts of the database a particular user would be allowed to get access to, and whether or not to allow an external program to access the network. Internal security is about ensuring that running programs are behaving themselves and not venturing into areas they shouldn't be in or executing processes they are restricted from doing (programs which are already loaded and appear to be safe are often a source of viruses through the Trojan horse method).

The above are all the functions of mainstream commercial operating systems of today. So at a technical level, that is what operating systems are all about. But Let's take our understanding of operating systems to a higher strategic level.

The Strategic Importance of Operating Systems

So from what we've said so far it appears that operating systems are really the 'behind the scenes' software without which the applications couldn't even begin to function. However, the task of choosing an operating system for a new company or a new venture is possibly one of the trickiest, most strategic decisions that an IT Director or Technical Architect is forced to make.

The choice of an operating system (from either of the 'open' or 'closed' families) can either set your organisation towards a path of smooth technological evolution in the years ahead, or result in a project rollout that's riddled with misery for your IT teams and continued conflict with your IT suppliers. The decision can make or break an organisation. Bill Gates realised very early in his career how strategically powerful operating systems could be. It also became abundantly clear to him that whoever controlled an all pervasive or ubiquitous operating system could go on to become a very powerful individual *indeed*.

Categorising Operating Systems

As mentioned in Chapter Three, operating systems can be separated into **two** important groupings, these are:

- Operating systems from the Unix family (and which are said to be '**open**') and

- Operating systems that are non-Unix (and said to be proprietary or '**closed**').

The battle lines have been drawn between these two opposing philosophies since the early eighties. And we need to understand why. In the next chapter we look at the first of these two groupings in more detail, and familiarise ourselves with the whole area of Unix.

Important Operating Systems Of Today

Unix
(And Unix-Like)

Proprietary
(And Closed-Source)

AIX
(From IBM)

Solaris
(From Sun)

A/UX
(From Apple Corporation)

HP-UX
(From Hewlett Packard)

Open BSD
(From University of California)

Darwin
(From Apple)

Tru64
(From Hewlett Packard)

Linux
Variants include:
Redhat
SuSe
Ubuntu
Mandriva
Debian
Gentoo

MS-DOS
(From Microsoft)

MacOS
(From Apple Corporation)

OS-390
(From IBM)

Z /OS
(From IBM)

Microsoft Windows Family

Includes:
Windows 95
Windows XP
Windows NT
Windows 2003
Windows Vista
Windows Mobile

CHAPTER FIVE

Recruiting Unix Specialists

Introduction

Many of the companies you speak to will have an infrastructure which is based squarely around a Unix platform; and consequently they will come to you with requirements for Unix administrators, and Unix engineers from all of the *flavours of Unix*. In this chapter we first acquaint ourselves with a brief history of the subject, which should give us a direct insight into why many organisations adopt the Unix OS; and an explanation into how all of these *flavours* came about. The benefits of this foundation knowledge will only truly manifest when you're discussing job specs with a client or in a face-to-face interview with a candidate. In the case of Unix this is particularly important because the actual *way* in which this particular technology came about contributed tremendously to the key strengths and characteristics of Unix today.

Unix and 'Space Travel' – A History

We don't need to go into an amazing amount of detail about the history of Unix but just enough to get you to realise the significance of Unix from a strategic perspective. Unix is huge – both as an IT concept but also in the impact it has had on the IT industry. This OS has secured its position in the IT Hall of Fame not simply as an IT paradigm, but also in the way it has affected the idea of how IT ideas can evolve and the notion of knowledge sharing. The story of Unix is inextricably linked with **AT&T Bell Laboratories** (the very same Bell labs we bumped into of the 'transistor' fame mentioned earlier in Chapter One).

Before Unix came along most operating systems were extremely large, and written in low-level assembly language. Each OS was **hardware-dependant** i.e. written specifically to work on only one particular type of machine. In the 1960s AT&T, **General Electric** and **MIT** started to work on an experimental operating system called **Multics** (Multiplexed Information and Computing Service) for use on an early mainframe. The resulting system was generally considered to be a poor product and eventually the project collapsed under the weight of its own complexities. But Unix was a significant concept that was to emerge out of that experience in an unexpected way.

Bell Labs lost heart in the whole operating system idea and pulled out of what they considered to be a doomed project. For them that was pretty much the end of the matter. However this left a very talented Bell employee, **Ken Thompson** (one of the original members of the Multics project), without a machine on which to play his beloved '**Space Travel**' game. Thompson had created his space-flight game during the Multics project to while away the more quiet moments (*as you do*). The game, though primitive by today's standards, simulated how a rocket might be navigated throughout the Solar System taking into account the gravity of planets etc. (PS. Just in case you're visualising some sort of graphical display with a fiery rocket and streaming space debris – forget it. This was a mathematical 'green screen' game driven by equations and calculations.) However, Thompson, now without the powerful hardware of the Multics project, had no way of surfing the asteroid belt in his spare time. Clearly something drastic would need to be done! **Therein lay the serious motivation for Unix!**

"When he walked into my office, I knew he was the perfect
geek to join our IT team. His shoelaces were USB cables."

Thompson spotted an abandoned minicomputer (**PDP-7** as shown below) gathering dust in a dark corner of Bell Labs and an idea started to form.

Along with his colleague **Dennis Ritchie** (acknowledged co-inventor of Unix and inventor of the C language), Thompson set about converting the computer into their own private Playstation!

But of course they needed a 'Multics-type' operating system that could sit on the abandoned machine to form the platform for their game. During this private project Thompson and Ritchie would learn much more about how to create operating systems that could be ported from one machine to another. **This was hugely important for the future of IT.**

Not only did they approach the whole idea of operating systems from a different angle; they also began to appreciate how important it would be for programmers in the future not to be tied down to creating operating systems that worked on just a single type of machine.

Figure 5.1
The PDP-7. The first machine to secretly house entertainment software, and forerunner to a generation of computers that would allow the user to appear to be working hard whilst playing games.

The First Steps Towards Portability

Unix soon came into being created using the C programming language. The first few versions of Unix were extremely clunky. As time went on however new hardware arrived on the scene at Bell laboratories. As each machine arrived, Thompson and Ritchie learned how to develop Unix so that it wouldn't have to be totally re-written for each of the new devices. Bell soon became impressed with the **portability** of Unix, and as word spread about his new OS which could be ported from machine to machine, the IT community too was beginning to take a keen interest in the new system.

The Computing Fellowship

The two programmers continued apace, implementing improvements to Unix, along with enhancements and modifications offered by others in the IT community. More significantly they also laid down the principal of a community of programmers who could take part in the process. Thus began the idea of a **'Computing Fellowship'** or **'communal computing'**.

The fellowship's key principal was:

"If people create something interesting in any field of IT, the rest of the IT community should be allowed to see how it works. In that way all interested parties can contribute, improve and help make it a better product."

This concept took off, and so by the mid-1970s Unix was distributed to universities and colleges and to the wider programming community. Programmers came out of the woodwork in their droves from educational, government and commercial institutions; who impatient with the limitations of existing systems, were happy to be able to suggest improvements, contribute to the new system and implement improvements which they felt were currently lacking. The seeds of the Unix movement were laid down.

Unix Flavours: A Family Affair

So to recap there was originally just a single **Unix** operating system, however today it is better to think of Unix as a *family* of operating systems which stem from that original *grandfather* Unix. All the members of this family conform to the original standard (specification) written for that first true Unix OS created in 1969. The Unix (or Unix-like) family includes

* Solaris
* Linux
* AIX
* HP-UX

These different Unix **flavours** (by the way it is perfectly acceptable to use the term 'flavour' when discussing Unix and with your clients or candidate) are all almost identical in their basic make-up, except for minor idiosyncrasies. Candidates will often be heard saying to you **'I'm a Unix bod'** which really means that *I specialise in looking after systems that are running on one of the members of the Unix family.* This has major implications both from a technical and recruitment perspective, as we shall see below.

Unix, Open-ness and Code Portability

As we've mentioned, the key thing about all of the Unix family members is that they are said to be **'open'. This is important.** It's a distinct trait which makes Unix such an important IT principal today.

'Open' software means that programmers have direct access to the source code and can see in minor detail exactly how the 'innards' of the software works.

No puns at this stage

Of course not all software is open, especially not the commercial offerings. The most famous software group deemed to be **closed** is of course the Microsoft family of operating systems. (At this juncture a lesser mortal would be tempted to bring in a plethora of corny puns relating to how in IT the Windows and Gates are always closed – but myself, I'm above such things.) We explore the nitty-gritty of closed or 'proprietary' operating systems in the next chapter.

Open Means 'Feel Free, Look inside'

Being 'open' means that users can actually flip open the bonnet of the application and tweak software such as Unix should they wish to do so. They can mend it when it goes wrong without asking permission from the vendor who sold it to them, and even attempt to improve it if they see flaws. The improvements can then be shared amongst the Unix community in the hope that the whole Unix community may subsequently benefit from their input.

The result of all of the above is that Unix is an operating system that has been constantly tweaked and modified over the last thirty years by people who class themselves as more adept than your average programmer. In fact one good **'barometer of geekiness'** is the response of your IT bod to the mere mention of the word 'Unix'. Many of the IT candidates who present themselves as jedi-level geeks will often validate their claims by declaring their undying love for Unix and explaining how they were amongst those who discussed and developed Unix in the 'open programming community'.

Summary: The Key Benefits of Unix

Because of the way in which it was created and subsequently developed on an ongoing basis by a community, Unix is

*   Open. Programmers can freely see and tweak the innermost source code (the kernel) without having to ask permission from the Unix creators.

*   Portable. Unix can be ported to newly developed computers, because it eliminates the need to re-write the OS from scratch.

*   Improvable. Unix is easy to customize and improve because it was

written in C, a language rapidly adopted by programmers around the world for that purpose.

- Loved. Because the 'fellowship' of Unix was responsible for its ongoing development, all the members of this fellowship feel as if they themselves were personally involved in its creation. For this reason Unix specialists are often quite attached to their OS and a slur upon it is considered to be a slur upon them personally.

Unix: A Recruitment Perspective

As a recruiter when you're looking for Unix specialists, another upshot of a Unix-based environment is that **Unix skill-sets are often transferable** too. So, although most clients will insist on you seeking out Unix administrators in a particular flavour such as (say) AIX, this also means that if resources were thin on the ground, you could possibly squeeze a Linux administrator to carry out that role. Depending on how desperate the client is they may, in many cases, consider this as a viable option.

Also, as a recruiter you must make it standard practice to ask your candidates, who specialise in one any of the Unix flavours (such as HP-UX, Solaris, Linux etc.), whether or not they would be able to switch to working with another Unix flavour if circumstances called for it. Most of them will shrug nonchalantly and explain that it wouldn't be too much of a bind; or as one of my candidates always explained in a low serious tone

"Hey, no big deal - Unix is Unix is Unix".

Recruiting Unix Today

Or Linux – The Penguin that Roared

One interesting repercussion of the Unix story is a system developed around the early 1990s by the name of Linux. It's worth mentioning here primarily because if you're recruiting Unix at the moment (2008 onwards), the 'golden boy' of the family is **Linux**. Most of your Unix candidates will be trying to master it. Many of your clients will be looking to adopt it as the Unix flavour of choice for their operation. Linux has established itself as one of the most popular open operating systems around today, and everything you read in this section will have a direct impact on the conversations you have with the candidates you speak to and the roles you recruit for.

Humble beginnings

The story of Linux is an intriguing one. In stark contrast to many other famous operating systems throughout history, Linux does not stem from the research lab of some mighty corporate IT powerhouse. The creation of Linux was chiefly driven by a talented programmer from Finland (who at the time was studying at the University of Helsinki) by the name of Linus Torvalds (whence he called his Unix flavour Linux – pronounced *Leenucks*).

Linux and the GNU Project

Torvalds was heavily influenced by and involved in the **GNU Project** whose principal aim (although it somewhat confusingly stands for **GNU's Not Unix**) was aimed at creating completely free versions of Unix. Remember, at the time, all of the Unix flavours of the day were *open* (i.e. you had access to the source code) but not necessarily *free of cost*. Torvalds wanted to put this right. He wanted to offer the world a flavour of Unix that could be downloaded for free off the Internet for personal use at home. It wasn't necessarily going to be as good as the perfectly polished paid-for versions of Unix, but hey, *what did you want for* **free**!

Unix for Free

So Linux became the world's first distribution of a truly free version of a Unix system (or 'Unix-like' to be more technically precise and to pander to the purists who may be reading this). The interesting thing to note at this point was that Torvalds never seemed to be in it for the money, or in order to take over the IT world. He didn't appear to be driven by an all-consuming commercial motivation, more by the spirit of open source development (you'll remember the 'fellowship' mentioned on page 66). It appears that he wanted you and I to be able to play around with Unix without having to have at our disposal the large corporate chequebooks normally associated with a Unix purchase.

How ironic then that today Linux is rapidly becoming the world leader amongst Unix flavours, the flavour of choice amongst the candidates and clients you speak to. And in another bizarre twist, Torvalds himself has ascended the ranks of the IT elite to such an extent that Linux is possibly the first amongst the Unix off-spring which Microsoft consider to be a worthy adversary in the cut-throat operating systems arena. So the question needs to be asked. How could Linus have managed to elevate his unassuming homespun OS to a position worthy of respect from the mighty Microsoft, when goliaths of the IT industry have previously failed to reach such lofty heights with their systems?

To a certain extent it does read a little (as Del Boy from *Only Fools and Horses* might put it) like the *parable of the lucky git*! But there was certainly more to it then that.

Here's how it happened.

Open Passion

Linus Torvalds pretty much started development of Linux in his bedroom on his home PC. He then shared it with friends and colleagues and then eventually put it onto the Internet chat rooms. At the time of launching Linux over the Internet (of course for free), Torvald attached only a few simple conditions which where

* Here it is. A free version of Unix, download it and enjoy. However If you find something wrong with it, let me know. Oh, and
* If you manage to make it work better in any way, do let me know so that I can pass the improvements on to everyone else.

(A copy of the original posting by Torvalds is shown below, the trigger for a revolution in IT which is still unfolding today). Torvalds clearly assumed at the time that only a few fellow programmers from the open source community might take some passing interest and download his free 'hobbyist' flavour of Unix. He might have also thought that a minority might even take the trouble to offer feedback on how to improve Linux. However it didn't quite work out that way. Something very unexpected happened.

Linux was about to feel the full passion and *power of open*.

THE ORIGINAL LINUS POSTING

```
25 Aug 91 20:57:08 GMT
Hello everybody out there using minix -

I'm doing a (free) operating system (just a hobby,
won't be big and professional like gnu) for 386(486)
AT clones.
This has been brewing since april, and is starting to
get ready. I'd like any feedback on things people
like/dislike in minix, as my OS resembles it somewhat
(same physical layout of the file-system (due to
practical reasons) among other things).

I've currently ported bash(1.08) and gcc(1.40), and
things seem to work. This implies that I'll get
something practical within a few months, and I'd like
to know what features most people would want. Any
suggestions are welcome, but I won't promise I'll
implement them :-)

                Linus (torvalds@kruuna.helsinki.fi)


PS. Yes - it's free of any minix code, and it has a
multi-threaded fs. It is NOT protable (uses 386 task
switching etc), and it probably never will support
anything other than AT-harddisks, as that's all I
have :-(.
```

Together We Can Make It

Initially take-up was slow. Only a few programmers downloaded the first version (version 0.01) of Linux in around 1992. That original version had a simple **kernel** (the core or heart of the program), which consisted of around 8400 lines of code.

Some programmers started to suggest improvements. So the kernel was modified. Then steady streams of suggestions started to come through, and were also implemented. By version 1.0 in 1994 the Linux kernel had grown to 170,000 lines of code. 'Impressive' thought Torvalds. But what happened from here was simply breathtaking. The open source programming community had only just started to take this seriously. *The Linux wagon had suddenly started to roll.*

The improvements would continue to flow in thick and fast for the next decade and beyond (in fact they continue to this day). So much so that by 2001 Linux version 2.4 had grown to become one of the (if not *the*) most impressive Unix flavours around, with a kernel of over **3 million lines** of code. Bizarrely, Linus Torvalds in his hands (and working from his university digs) held the rights to possibly the most powerful flavour of Unix on the planet; developed by programmers who were contributing to it with such a frenzy that possibly even Bill Gates might have had to think twice at the time about the development cost of such a project... and Torvalds was getting it done *for free.*

In fact a recent study (carried out by Red Hat) relating to later versions of Linux showed that actually around **55 million lines** of code went backwards and forwards during its development and an estimated **eight thousand man-years** of development time were notched up. *Years!*

At that time, if you had initiated this exercise commercially in the US using contracted programmers, you would have had to pay in excess of 1.9 billion dollars to develop Linux.

'Paid-for' Linux

Undoubtedly Linux had become an amazing operating system. It was acknowledged as such globally after having passed numerous commercial trials. But of course no matter how good it seemed, no large commercial organisation was going to adopt Linux unless it had a proper vendor support structure behind it. So in 1993 companies such as **SuSe**, **Redhat** and **Debian** were formed. These were the commercial Linux distributors or '**distro**s'. Companies that offered **paid-for versions of Linux** which would be supported commercially just like any other purchased software. Suddenly Linux took off in the commercial environment as many companies decided to dump their existing OS to come over to 'supported Linux'.

By 2006 there were well over 200 Linux distributors.

Summary

Today Linux continues to grow apace, and has been widely implemented as the OS for enterprise architectures around the world. It has also found strategic alliance with notables such as IBM, Compaq and HP all of who are happy to promote 'Tux' the penguin (see logo below). Linux is also at the heart of the operating for many Internet Service Providers (ISP) and now also boasts an increasing range of application software many of which are free. It is the one flavour of Unix which you as a recruiter need to keep an eye on. Candidates who have this skillset need to be looked after and marketed out very quickly to any large client who uses Unix.

"Some people have told me they don't think a fat penguin really embodies the grace of Linux, which just tells me they have never seen an angry penguin charging at them in excess of 100mph. They'd be a lot more careful about what they say if they had."
-- Linus Torvalds

Quick Glance Summary

UNIX SUMMARY SHEET

Key Points

- Created by Ken Thompson and Dennis Ritchie in 1969
- Whilst they were working at Bell Laboratories
- Unix was the first OS that was designed to be portable across machines
- Laid down the foundation for 'Computing Fellowship' or 'Open-ness' in

Core Principles

- Unix-based systems are generally open source which means that programmers have access to the code
- All Unix-like operating systems function in a similar way at their core
- Unix-based applications that were created to work on one flavour of Unix can generally be ported to another with minor tweaking
- All manufacturers of hardware generally have their own Unix based operating system
- This means that if you change hardware vendor, you wont have to re-write your expensive applications.
- Because you can see the source code of your Unix OS, you aren't locked in to any company to ask permission to make changes.

What we should see on their CV

There are over fifty Unix-like flavours on the market today, but some of the more popular ones in the IT industry are

- Linux (Linus Torvalds)
- Solaris (Sun)
- HP-UX (Hewlett Packard)
- AIX (IBM)
- Tru64 (formally Digital Unix)
- SCO Unix (Santa Cruz Operations)

CHAPTER SIX

Understanding Closed IT Systems

An Overview

Having given considerable emphasis to Unix and open systems in Chapter Five, it seems only fair to spend some time discussing the virtues of proprietary systems. They too have their unique selling points. As previously mentioned, proprietary operating systems are those which are promoted by software manufacturers who do not want external programmers to freely see how the source code operates. For this reason proprietary software is also referred to as being '**closed**'.

Companies which work under this model do so for a number of reasons, not least so that they can protect their products from piracy, virus attack and of course duplication by competitors through reverse engineering.

STRAIGHT TO

➤ Proprietary
Systems
Page 78

➤ What this means
for recruiters
Page 80

➤ The Microsoft
Family
Page 81

"It might be some sort of evolution thing.
Your baby's navel is an Ethernet port."

Examples of Proprietary Operating Systems

Closed systems include

- The Windows Family (From Microsoft)
- MacOS (From Apple)
- OS39 (From IBM)

Deploying Closed Operating Systems

The key implications of adopting a closed approach is that, when a company commits to running its IT system in a closed environment, one never has complete knowledge of the intricate way in which the software functions at its deepest level – so there will always be a tendency for you to rely on the vendor of that system for all of your low-level support *for as long as that system is in place.* Bearing this in mind some in the IT community feel that, with closed systems, you could consign yourself to a future of total dependency on a third party; especially if the implementation of that system meant a huge financial investment in the first place.

Another ramification of adopting a closed OS is that your **applications** are limited to use only with that OS. Generally if you develop application software for your closed platform, they will not subsequently be easily portable across to another operating system at some point in the future (unlike the Unix scenario). This has huge implications financially since development of bespoke commercial software is usually a costly exercise and not one to be taken lightly. If one did feel like changing vendors at any point in the future, you would then have to make the painful decision between re-writing all of your applications from scratch … or staying put. Because of the considerable costs associated with the re-writing of applications, many companies opt for the latter option.

The Benefits of A Closed Operating System

There must be some key benefits, of course, in going down the closed software road; and we'll explore these now. They are perceived to be as follows:

- Firstly, it could be argued that since closed software is primarily driven by commercial motives; their evolution is urged along by vigorous market forces, which continually push them to always strive towards excellence.

- Secondly, these same market forces urge continuous adaptation of the product in order to outwit the competition and/or the malicious hacker – thus resulting in a better leading-edge product which (in theory) should also be more secure and stable.

- Thirdly, and maybe most importantly, the company which produces closed commercial products will have to employ excellent marketing, promotion and general awareness of their product. For this reason commercially motivated products will probably be more widely recognised than those that don't have a mega-corporation cracking the whip behind them. Very few of the everyday visitors to a shopping mall will know what a Unix logo looks like, or who Ken Thompson was (page 64 for a reminder). However there will be very few who don't recognise the Windows logo or who have never heard of Bill Gates.

- And finally; most successful software applications are invariably closed and are built to sit on closed operating systems. It simply makes commercial sense. Software houses develop applications primarily to make money. By definition therefore, software companies will initially market their software towards the most widely used operating systems in the market – such as MS Windows. So if my company or I need the best 'Off The Shelf' (**OTS**) software (i.e. MS Office, Photoshop, CorelDraw etc.) then a safe bet is to go out and buy a machine that operates using the market's leading operating system (whatever that happens to be).

The Open and Closed Argument Rages on

In many ways this open/closed battle has formed the backdrop to the IT industry since the birth of the Internet and the subsequent rise in knowledge sharing. Both sides have a strong case, but nowhere else in IT does the debate get so passionately contested, at an almost emotional level.

There will always be those from within the open movement who vehemently despise the closed software vendors with zeal, labelling them 'money grabbing control freaks'. Similarly there are those from the closed camp who view the open community as a bunch of open-sandalled hippies with no real business acumen. This group sees no harm whatsoever in creating an innovative environment that also rewards individuals and corporations financially. The proprietary vendors cannot conceive of a software industry that has to rely on code that has been tinkered and played about with by all and sundry.

Summary

What This Means for you as a Recruiter

As a recruiter you will generally find that the network administrators, network engineers and even the network managers you recruit will fall into those from a Unix background and those from a closed background. Candidates who class themselves as Unix Administrators will seldom wish to get involved in looking after a Windows environment and vice versa. You will also be able to categorise your *clients* as broadly leaning either towards a 'Unix' platform or 'proprietary' platform. It is therefore essential that you get to understand the key characteristics associated with each category and why your clients might side with one or the other.

Opposite is a summary sheet outlining the major operating systems within the Microsoft family.

The Microsoft Family of Operating Systems

MS- DOS
Created in 1981 for the first range of IBM PCs.

Windows 3.11
This was the most successful version of the early windows versions. Windows 1.0 and Windows 2.0 did exist but Windows 3.11 ironed out much of the weaknesses of its predecessors.

Windows For Workgroups

Windows NT
Released in July 1993 as the company's first true stab at an OS which could control business-level client-server networks.

Windows 95 Released in August 1995.

Windows 98   Released in June 1998.

Windows ME Released in September 2000.

Windows XP Merging many features of Windows NT/95 and 98.

Windows 2000 Released in February 2000 for the server market.

Windows Vista Released in November 2006.

Windows Server 2008
Released in February 2008 and brings together all of the strengths of Vista into a networked environment.

PART 3

UNDERSTANDING THE
IT PROJECT LIFECYCLE

CHAPTER SEVEN

An Overview of the IT Project Lifecycle

Introducing the IT Project Lifecycle

"The other stuff was good...but that... that was it! That really gets to the heart of what we are about as recruiters!"

I still hear it time and again during the training courses, but it became apparent to me very quickly. There is one chunk of knowledge which will always have a jaw-dropping effect on the new recruiters whom I teach. That piece of knowledge is the IT project lifecycle. Once you understand this, you simply cease to be an ordinary recruiter.

"The secret to happiness is: Always get as much RAM as you can possibly afford."

So What is the IT Project Lifecycle?

The IT project lifecycle is a structured approach which many companies turn to when they are developing new software or rolling out new IT systems. You'll also hear it being referred to as the '**software development lifecycle**' or the '**Waterfall Model**'.

You will often hear clients asking for candidates who

"Have had exposure to the full project lifecycle".

For many of your clients, their IT recruitment process will be dictated by this approach. It defines the urgency of their recruitment needs, which roles are needed, the approximate duration of each contract, and the sequence of hiring. The project lifecycle drives the recruitment process of your clients and is therefore at the heart your activities too, which is why we'll discuss the topic fully in this chapter.

Before you can begin to absorb the IT roles in detail it is critical to understand where in the project lifecycle each role makes an appearance and what is required of them at that stage.

This chapter is hugely relevant to your understanding of IT recruitment.

How the Idea of Structured Development Came About

In the very early days of IT, the use of computers and software applications (and I use the term 'applications' in the loosest possible sense!) was very much limited to scientific research and academic pursuits. In these early days of IT, there simply wasn't the tremendous financial pressure to produce efficient, cost-effective applications that would yield payback for investment. As a result there wasn't the onus on the developers of those early applications to lay down standards of excellence, or even a particular method or procedure for programming in an efficient manner.

Development in the early days was largely haphazard and very little strategic thought went into how IT might be exploited to its fullest commercial extent. And because nobody immediately appreciated the potential link between IT and business, software development remained the pastime of a small (yet growing) number of early pseudo-scientific 'techies'.

The result of course was a first generation of notably underwhelming applications. Those fledgling programs were poorly tested, poorly documented, with bugs running rampant throughout the reams of code. However, even so, those clumsy early attempts at software development would nonetheless form the 'primordial software ooze' from which all future programs would evolve.

Let's Bring Some Order to this Party

In the 1960s, however, more and more business corporations were beginning to appreciate the potential benefits that computers might bring, and around this time the UK's **National Computer Centre** (NCC) developed what many acknowledge as the first structured approach to the process of creating software applications. Their thinking went a bit like this:

1. Today's programs are generally a bit rubbish. They may be okay for the research labs but have no place in business. Why? Because

2. There is no real analysis of the problem from a *business perspective*. It may well be that the way a problem *manifests* in a program is actually not the root cause of the problem itself but may stem from a poor business process. So

3. We need to spend more time gathering facts about the problem *from a business perspective*. And then maybe

4.   This would help us define a 'good' system' in comparison to the 'poor system' that we have now. So **benchmarks** could be assigned to allow us to determine whether the new system we're creating is an improvement or not. We could then set about

5.   Designing our new software product in order to yield improvements. And then

6.   We could actually start physical programming of code in a systematic way.

7.   Finally the program could be tested and implemented.

In short the formal stages the NCC came up with were

*   Planning

*   Analysis

*   Design

*   Development

*   Implementation

And so for this reason this model was often referred to as the **PADDI** approach. This can be thought of as the forerunner to most modern day structured approaches.

The Waterfall Model

Shortly after this, around 1970, an American software engineer named **Winston Royce** released the idea of the 'Waterfall Model' in a white paper to tackle the lack of structure in programming. Ironically, as we shall see later on, the waterfall approach was not actually the one Royce was advocating in the technical paper. He much preferred the **Iterative Approach**, which he outlined in the second half of the same paper (see Chapter 8). Most of the readers of his work however were rather more impressed by the 'pretty picture' which illustrated his first theory and because it looked like a pleasant waterfall – and so bizarrely that was the approach that took off, much to the consternation of Royce!

Today, the waterfall model can be thought of as being synonymous with any structured IT project rollout. There are many variations to this approach, with some having additional phases, whilst others are simpler, but generally **the term waterfall model can be applied to any structured and sequential approach to development**. When you speak to clients they will often refer to themselves as operating in either a 'structured' environment or an 'iterative' (which we shall tackle later).

I'd like to reiterate again, that once you are aware of the various approaches, as used by many IT departments around the world, you cease to be just another ordinary recruiter; and the veil of mystery with regards the recruitment process has been lifted as you begin to see IT recruitment from the viewpoint of your client's IT department.

Note: In the following chapter I'll be using the terms 'waterfall', 'lifecycle' and 'structured' in an almost interchangeable manner. This is what your clients will do too, so why not start getting you used to it here.

So, let's go there now without further ado…

Ladies and gentlemen I present …

The Waterfall Model (or Project Lifecycle)

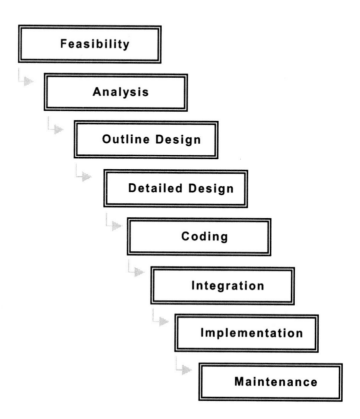

Figure 7.1
The Project
Lifecycle.

How IT Roles Appear in the Lifecycle

At each stage of the lifecycle different roles start to 'kick in'. They 'do their thing', pass their results to the next person down the waterfall and then usually move away from the project.

BIG HINT: In fact whenever you are given a role to recruit for, you already have a significant hint as to where in the lifecycle your client's project is at, and therefore you may even be able to pre-empt the following roles which might be required in a few short months.

As you can see in this approach the rollout is broken down into a number of sequential stages. In its original form the model had eight stages however, as previously mentioned, in recent times the term 'Waterfall Model' is taken to mean any sequential model that follows this general approach; regardless of the number of stages. An interesting aspect of this model is that the *output* from one stage forms the *input* for the next stage. The project lifecycle won't flow properly unless each stage is completed correctly. So, in the form that I describe above, for example, **Detailed design** cannot proceed without **Outline design** having been completed satisfactorily. Similarly **coding** cannot proceed at all if either of the above has not been executed to completion.

It's also worth noting that in a poorly executed waterfall-based rollout there is often not a great deal of interaction between the stages apart from the transfer of data. This often leads to inherent problems with this way of working and so some IT projects began to favour alternative approaches that were subsequently put forward (we'll discuss these later on in this chapter). But for now let's take a look at what each of these stages really mean in laymen's terms, and also take a first swoop at introducing the IT role titles to you, starting with...

The Feasibility Stage

This is the initial stage which triggers most IT projects. The resulting documentation from this phase of the process will indicate to the IT Director as to whether or not it's worth actually proceeding with a new IT project in the first place.

Note: No technical answers are being sought at this stage. We are simply speaking to the users in order to define the current problems and identify whether the need for a new system is there, and whether or not the potential costs are justified. This stage is carried out by the **Business Analyst** (or in some cases the Systems Analyst or Information Analyst).

The details of what happens during this stage and the role of the Business Analyst (BA) are discussed in much more detail in Chapter 12.

Carrying Out the Feasibility Stage

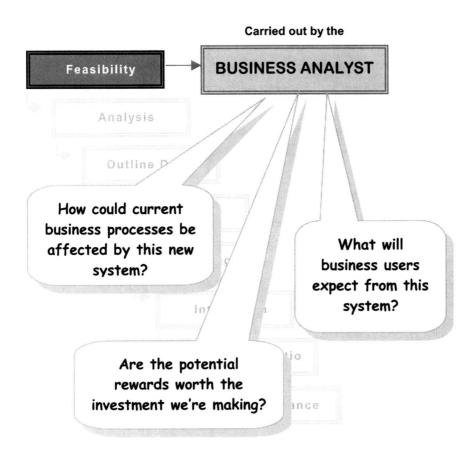

Figure 7.2
Business Analyst in
the Project Lifecycle

This role is
discussed in detail in
Chapter 10.

The BA has said 'Yes'... Hire a Project Manager!

Once we have the go ahead for the project from the results of our feasibility study, a Project Manager is immediately recruited (unless you have a permanent PM on site already) to take on the rest of the team and to ensure that the project is monitored and managed with regard to time constraints, financial accountability and resource management. PMs are very special people. They have the people skills to motivate individuals on the team, and ensure that all of the teams are working towards key milestones.

The role of a Project Manager and Programme Manager are both thoroughly discussed in Chapter 10.

Bringing on the Project Manager

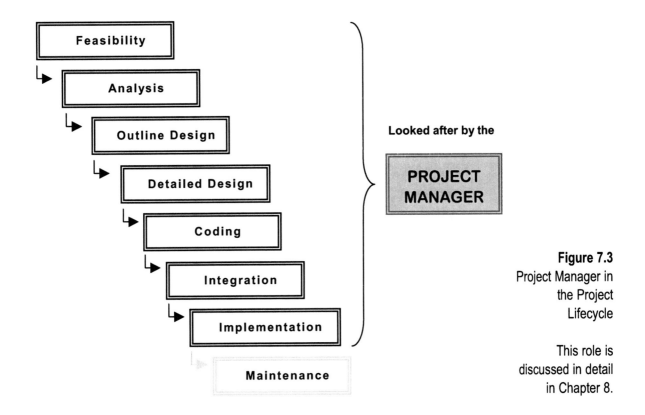

Figure 7.3
Project Manager in
the Project
Lifecycle

This role is
discussed in detail
in Chapter 8.

The Analysis Stage

The analysis stage is one in which most of the focus goes into defining the technical hurdles which might need to be faced. Again this is not the stage at which detailed solutions are thought out by a technical genius. That needs to wait a bit longer. During this stage the Systems Analyst (SA) will spend time and effort on analysing how data flows around the business, and how a new IT system might affect business processes. Around this stage there is a great focus on creating data models, which is one of the key activities for all Systems Analysts.

The analysis stage and the role of the Systems Analyst (SA) are fully discussed in much more detail in Chapter 12.

Carrying out the Analysis Stage

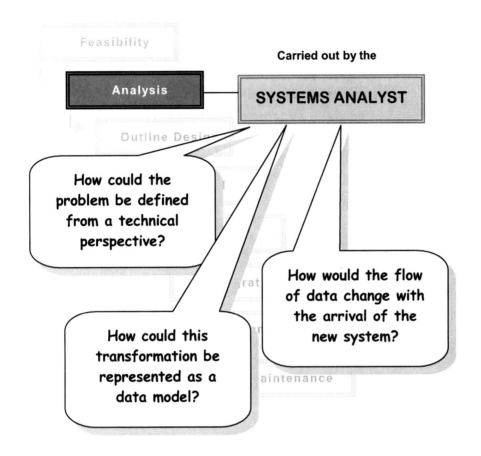

Figure 7.4
Systems Analyst in
the Project Lifecycle

This role is
discussed in detail in
Chapter 10.

The Design Stage

This is the stage at which all of the technical wizardry takes place. And so by implication this is the stage during which the brainiest technical gurus set their minds to the tasks involved. Problems need to be tackled, inspired solutions need to be brought to bear, blueprints need to be drawn up so that programmers can eventually be brought together in order to build code. This stage is the realm of the Technical Architect.

This stage and the Technical Architect (TA) role are both discussed in much more detail in Chapter 11.

Carrying out the Design Stage

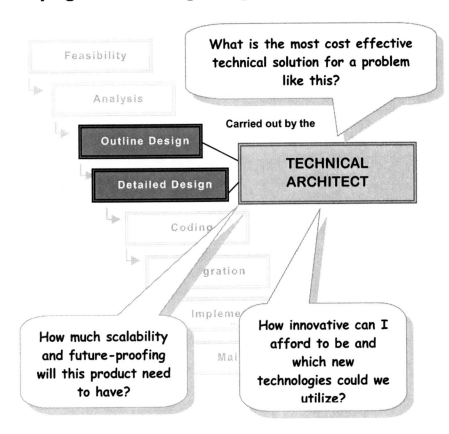

Figure 7.5
Technical Architects in the Project Lifecycle

This role is discussed in detail in Chapter 9.

The Coding Stage

Having received the technical specification document (also referred to as the blueprint) from the TA, the developers can then get to work on building the program (don't worry at this stage about the different titles relating to developers, programmers etc. We'll discuss these properly in later chapters).

The coding stage is where the ideas in the technical specification are transformed into physical working code that must actually *do* something. Teams of programmers assemble millions of lines of C++, Java and VB.NET; and what started off as a mere idea at the early stages of the lifecycle now starts to take shape as a working solution.

This entire area of languages, software development and the role of developers (in their various guises) is discussed in much more detail in Chapters 13–18.

Carrying out the Coding Stage

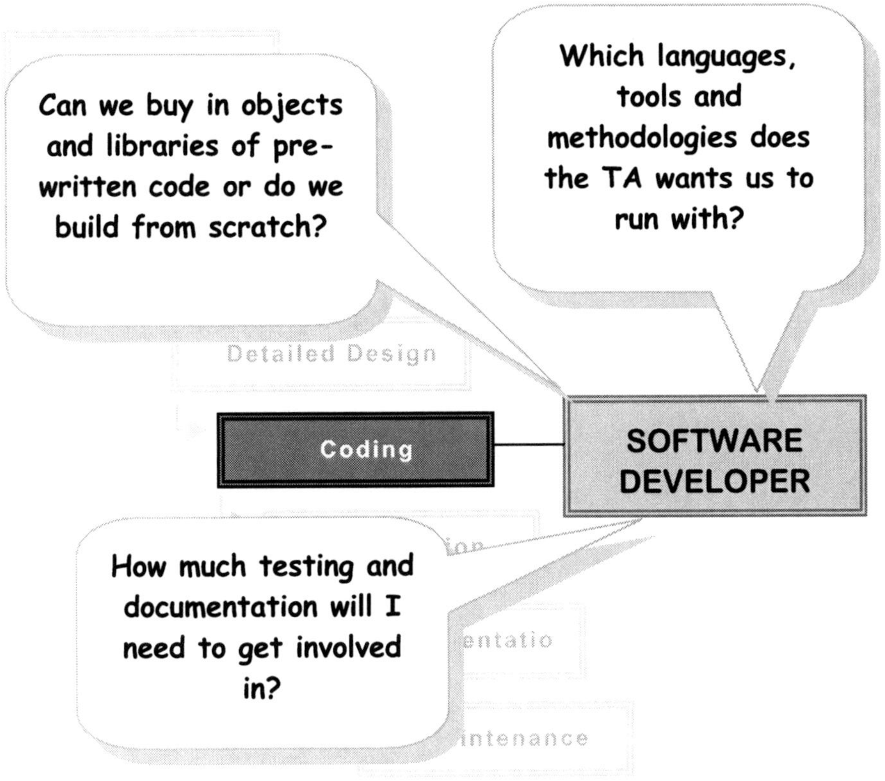

Can we buy in objects and libraries of pre-written code or do we build from scratch?

Which languages, tools and methodologies does the TA wants us to run with?

Detailed Design

Coding

SOFTWARE DEVELOPER

How much testing and documentation will I need to get involved in?

Figure 7.6
Software Developers in the Project Lifecycle

This role is discussed in detail in Chapters 11 to 17.

The Integration and Implementation Stages

Of course, once the code has been assembled into something approaching a final product, it will all need to be thoroughly tested before delivery to the end user. This is a tense and frustrating stage of the lifecycle; all of the product flaws and failings are rooted out.

There are numerous testing roles with an associated plethora of tools and terminology. Recruiting testers is a specialist area in itself and we'll take a good look at the major aspects of this role in Chapter 18.

Carrying out the Integration and Implementation Stage

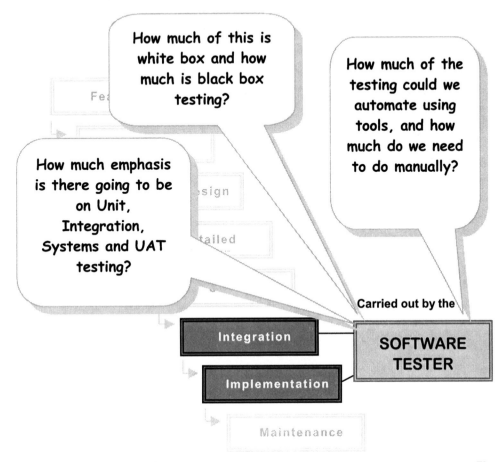

Figure 7.7
Software Testers in
the Project Lifecycle

This role is
discussed in detail in
Chapter 18.

The Maintenance Stage

You, the reader, are currently in the Maintenance Stage of your Waterfall Model with the software which you use on a daily basis. At this stage the so-called 'complete and fully-functioning' software has been installed onto your system and is being fully used in a live environment. Of course when things go wrong we need to call on the services of the people in IT Support and Systems Administration to help us.

We discuss IT Support roles in much more detail in Chapter 20.

Carrying out the Maintenance Stage

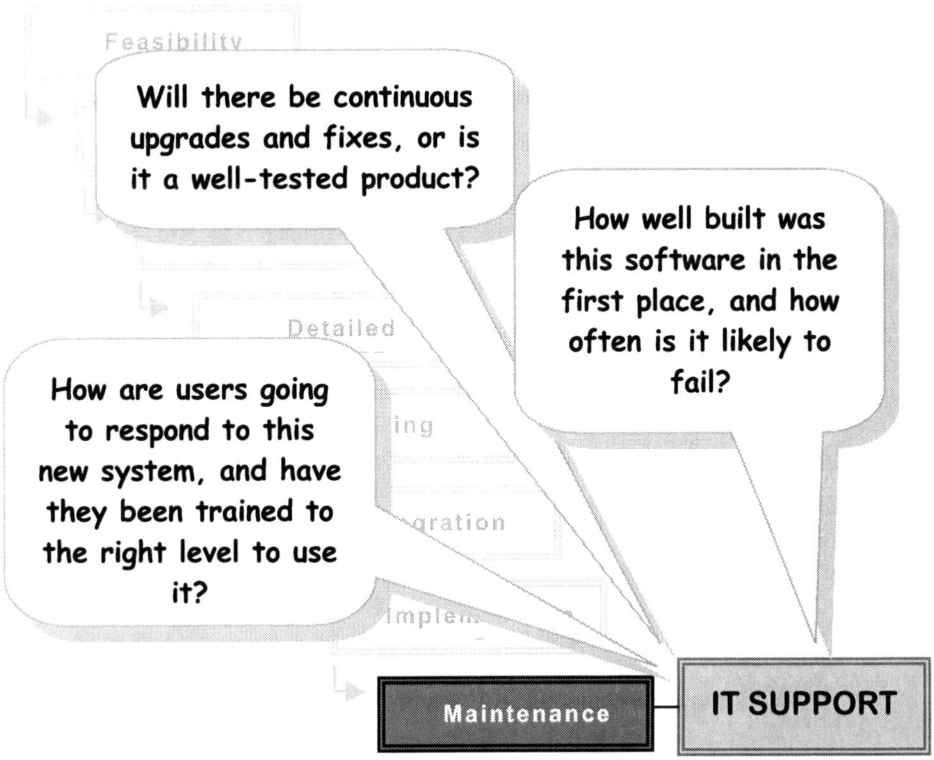

Figure 7.8
IT Support in the
Project Lifecycle

This role is
discussed in detail in
Chapter 20.

Structured Systems Analysis and Design (SSADM)

A variation of the waterfall model is the **Structured Systems Analysis and Design Methodology** (or **SSADM**) and is a term which you will see regularly appearing on CVs or job specs. This approach was created in the UK by the government's Central Computer and Telecommunications Agency (CCTA), and is often the de facto methodology taught to most rookie programmers entering the field, and especially to those working in the public sector.

SSADM (being, at the time of printing, at version 4.3 and now called SSADM 4+) has **six stages.** Once again, each stage needs to be completed before the next stage can be tackled. Because of its Civil Service roots it too has been criticised for being too procedural and bureaucratic, however SSADM does provide for the use of prototyping (preparing a working model). This means that there is more flexibility and scope for change within SSADM in comparison to the purist form of the Waterfall Model.

The stages within SSADM are as follows: start with Stage 0 as the Feasibility study. The stages

*   **Stage 0: Feasibility Study**. This is called Stage 0 because it isn't thought to be compulsory, and assumes that some projects are deemed to go ahead regardless. In this stage a **Problem Definition Statement** and a **Feasibility Study** report is created.

*   **Stage 1: Investigate Current Environment**. Very similar to the analysis stage of the Waterfall Model, the current system is observed and documented using dataflow diagrams and Entity Relationship Models (see page 193 for an understanding of these).

*   **Stage 2: Business System Options**. This is the stage at which a number of potential solutions (with their associated costs) will be put forward to the users, and they will be asked to choose one of the options to carry forward into development.

- **Stage 3: Requirements Specification.** The favoured option from stage 2 is now clearly defined and described in detail.

- **Stage 4: Technical Systems Options.** At this stage the users are asked in more technical detail the manner in which they would like the system to be implemented.

- **Stage 5: Logical Design.** At this stage the technical experts take their first crack at putting together a solution outline based on all of their findings so far.

- **Stage 6: Physical Design.** Finally this involves the actual programming of the code and assessing performance of parts of the new system.

Summary

So we're now on the road at last! We're actually at a stage where IT role titles are starting to be bandied around merrily in their own right. You'll also have noticed that 'The Guide' won't allow us to take any of the roles lightly or just discuss them merely in passing. In 'The Guide' we have entire chapters dedicated to the various skill sets and key IT roles which you will encounter during your career.

In summary we've said that there are many advantages in using the IT project lifecycle approach to building IT systems, however as I've indicated in the summary sheet below, it has its flaws too. And so, unsurprisingly, it isn't the only approach which your clients will adopt when embarking on a software development project. So for now I want to carry on and clarify the alternative approaches to IT development which you should also be aware of. These alternative schools of thought also have a corresponding influence on the IT recruitment processes of the companies which adopt them.

But for now 'The Guide' marches on and beckons us to follow.

We are getting closer to understanding the various candidates who will present themselves to you. But first we need to be aware that not all of your clients will base their recruitment around the IT project lifecycle approach. With this in mind, let's get into the next chapter and further our understanding of the alternative approaches which your clients may adopt.

Advantages & Disadvantages of the Waterfall Approach

Strengths	Weaknesses
The sequence of activities is clear and well-defined.	Estimating costs and time is still difficult for each stage.
Each stage is easy to validate and so more open to verification and monitoring.	Users have no input in the way the software is developed for much of the process.
The clear structure of rollout ensures a level of quality and benchmarking at each stage.	There is little scope for prototyping (experimenting with a working model).
The structure is Project Management friendly in terms of defining success and completion of each stage.	Waterfall models can take, on average, two years to deliver the final product.
There is usually enough time set aside for such projects that products are adequately tested prior to delivery.	The final product when given to the user is often out of date and of no real value in their current market.

CHAPTER EIGHT

Recruiting for Agile and RAD Environments

Introduction

There are of course a number of alternatives to the widely accepted Waterfall Model. Although some of your clients will use approaches (such as SSADM) which are not the same as but loosely based around the waterfall method, other clients might adopt approaches (such as AGILE) which shun the project lifecycle idea completely due to its inherent weaknesses and disadvantages.

In this chapter I'll bring to your attention some of the alternative approaches which you will see appearing on cvs; primarily with the aim of making you realise that the strategy your clients apply to their recruitment process will vary tremendously depending on which camp they fall into.

Let's look at the first of these now.

STRAIGHT TO

➤ Iterative approaches and RAD
  Page 110

➤ The Spiral Model
  Page 112

➤ The Agile approach
  Page 113

➤ Summary sheet
  Page 115

"Frankly sir, we're tired of being
on the cutting edge of technology."

The Iterative Approaches to IT Development

Or 'I'm just MAD about RAD!'

Bearing in mind the apparent disadvantages of following a sequential, structured approach, there was always a distinct need to come up with new ways of thinking regarding the rollout of an IT system. Many of the IT departments who recruit from you will religiously follow a structured approach; however others will opt for the alternative model. **Iterative approaches** are less structured, more flexible and are based around the immediate needs of the user.

The principal theme around which most iterative approaches revolve is the creation of a rough working model or **prototype of the software very early on in the project**. This prototype is then presented to the users who then have an input into its ongoing development. As the users feedback on the various stages of the development the model is modified in *iterations* (small increments which hone in on the final solution). This approach has obvious benefits, as we shall soon see, and in the following pages we take a good look at a number of these iterative approaches.

Rapid Application Development

Rapid Application Development (or **RAD**) has become a popular alternative to the structure approaches. The principal behind RAD is to get a system created *quickly* (surprise, surprise!). However one of the other big benefits is to **involve end-users** by means of workshops and **prototyping** (creating a working model very quickly).

One great benefit of RAD is that it very quickly allows end-users to establish close links with the team of experts involved in the development. They work together and consult at regular intervals. After consultation with the users the team of experts (the **Joint Application Development** or **JAD** team) works in staged delivery by presenting a working prototype to the users. As they gather feedback from the users, they are able to chip away at the working model and slowly eliminate obvious weaknesses whilst at the same time implementing key features. This process is known as '**iterative prototyping**'. Of course, all of the above has to be done within a strict time frame too. With RAD projects the over-riding concern is often speed to market, and so the whole thing is often dictated by the urgency factor. So much so that each stage of prototype development operates within an agreed period known as a '**time box**'. At the end of each time box additional functionality continues to be added to the basic prototype. And as each time box expires, more and more 'nice to have' features appear.

The great advantage of this approach of course is that users are able to reap immediate benefits far earlier than if they were involved in a Waterfall approach. With RAD, users **might even come the conclusion surprisingly early on** in the iterations (and well within the expected budget) that one of the very early prototypes pretty much did just what they wanted the product to do, and it wouldn't be worthwhile proceeding any further. With the Waterfall model this should never happen since the users would have to wait for the entire lifecycle to work through to completion before seeing anything tangible.

Advantages and Disadvantages of RAD

RAD is very suited to particular situations, specifically:

- If there is an over-riding need for fast delivery (for example when bringing a new idea or concept to the marketplace).

- If there is a culture of user involvement within software development.

- If users are hesitant or unwilling to commit to a detailed definition relating to the final product.

On the other hand RAD has disadvantages too, and is usually not an approach suited to the following situations:

- RAD is not generally suited to large and complex IT end products, especially if the final item is a mission-critical system upon which the entire business will rely.

- In situations where the software needs to be fully tested in a variety of scenarios and is required to be (as near as possible) perfectly stable and robust. So RAD would not be ideally suited for development in sectors such as health, defence or any life-critical or mission-critical systems.

- Finally, if there is a danger of user involvement creating un-reasonably high levels of expectation from the final product, or where there is no apparent end to the enhancements and changes put forward by the users.

The Spiral Model

Another iterative approach created by W.W. Royce (he of the Waterfall Model fame) is known as the Spiral Model. This was one of the first methodologies to focus on an iterative way of working and is therefore heavily prototype based. Like the Waterfall Model it had stages but it also allowed the development team to go back over those stages to continue improvements – several times if necessary.

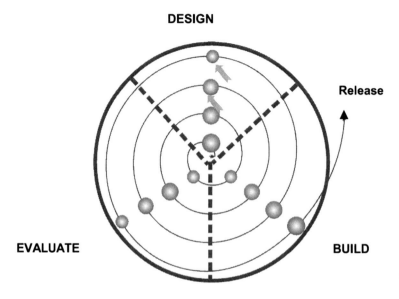

173

The Agile Approach

Two more terms often seen cropping up on CVs and job descriptions with increasing rapidity are **Agile** and **Extreme** programming. The 'Agile' method (or strictly speaking '*family* of methods') was yet another move by the software industry around the mid-1990s to counteract the structured approaches of the day.

One of the early pioneers of this approach was a technique known as **Extreme Programming**, though this was by no means the first of the Agile methods.

The Agile approach is (to all extents and purposes) iterative and targeted the following issues:

•   Software needs to be delivered quickly.

•   Software needs to be tweaked continuously in line with the users needs.

•   Cooperation and face-to-face communication between users and developers is critical.

•   Producing working software quickly is what is truly important.

Rational Unified Process

The final method I'd like to introduce, again because it continues to appear on CVs, is an iterative approach known as the **Rational Unified Approach** (or **RUP**). This was developed by a company called Rational Software in the early 1980s, though the company has changed hands many times since then. Once again this approach aims to overcome the flaws of the structured approach and its appearance on your candidates CVs will imply that they are heavily oriented towards a RAD or iterative approach.

Summary and Recruitment Perspective

With all of your clients, you need to be aware of whether they are operating in a 'structured' (Waterfall, SSADM etc.) environment or whether they prefer a more iterative approach to their software development projects. And this has a huge impact on how they recruit. You could simply ask the client, however you should also now (with your new-found knowledge) be able to figure it out for yourself from the methodologies and technologies which they mention on their job descriptions.

Similarly with candidates, you should be able to tell, from the methodologies and approaches which they have used in the past, as to whether they are more suited to a RAD or structured environment. The likelihood is that candidates who have previously worked in a RAD environment will want to continue in a fast moving time-sensitive development theatre of war. On the other hand 'waterfall' or 'lifecycle' people tend to be less concerned with being parachuted into a hectic, fast-moving war zone where the pressure is always on. They are often more happy in being able to focus diligently on their own well-defined area of work for eight hours a day, to then clock off and head back home.

A tip is to look at their fingernails. Well manicured and perfectly maintained digits implies someone who heads off at 5.30pm on the dot to the bosom of their family (definitely Waterfall); whereas fingernails that have been nervously bitten down to the nub and are tainted an intense shade of nicotine brown suggests '*I'm just mad about RAD!*'

Quick Glance Summary

Iterative Development Approaches

Core Principles

- **While there are many benefits in using the structured approaches, they have their down sides...**

  So a number of approaches were developed to quickly bring software products to the market or to the user base. These approaches focus on speed of development and user involvement, which usually means that the end product will meet current needs.

Associated Concepts

- **RAD** (Rapid Application Development)

  Spiral (Keep revising the product until it meets your needs)

  Prototyping (Creating a model quickly for users to feedback on)

  Agile (A group of Iterative approaches)

  RUP (Rational Unified Process)

Recruitment Perspective

  Your clients will refer to themselves as being either 'structured' or 'iterative' in the way they develop software. From this you can take a good guess as to how they will carry out their recruitment process. 'Structured' or 'Waterfall' means that they will take on different roles at timely intervals one after the other – and we can pre-empt this sequence with our new found knowledge of the waterfall model. An iterative or RAD approach will mean a more fluid approach in recruitment, often requiring many roles at the same time.

PART

4

RECRUITING
SENIOR IT ROLES

CHAPTER NINE

Recruiting IT Directors

Introduction

So we finally crack on with the roles – and you've landed the big one – well done! It can often take months of heavily-saccharined phone calls, numerous games of golf played with a suitably crooked 5-iron, and umpteen lavish meals before even the best executive search consultants in the business can snare such a prized role. What you have undertaken to do in no uncertain terms is to recruit the head honcho within the IT department. This is the pinnacle of the IT food chain, certainly from a strategy and planning perspective. And, as the title implies, the buck certainly stops here.

WHY ARE WE DOING THIS?

"It's not a great mission statement, but we'll revise it if things get better."

All strategic decisions are ultimately made at this level, and responsibility for all poor decisions also comes to rest on this person's shoulders too. However, it may surprise you to know that IT Directors are not necessarily renowned (or even hired) for their technical expertise. Even so they find themselves mapping out the IT strategy for entire corporations and subsequently justifying their actions to the company's board and shareholders. This person wields an immense amount of influence, and if you are lucky enough to be able to build a strong working relationship with them in due course, be prepared for much more business coming your way as new projects start to take shape.

Lets take a closer look at the role of the IT Director.

"That's our new mission statement."

The Role in Detail

Key Responsibilities

Broadly speaking IT Directors must;

•   Be able to create a VISION.

•   Have outstanding leadership qualities.

•   Be cautiously receptive to innovation.

•   Be able to create a PLAN.

•   Be able to motivate the real money people.

•   Be very well connected within the industry.

•   Be able to ultimately take full responsibility.

I've refer you back to our schematic representation of the IT department on page 123, to remind you just what an awesome responsibility the IT Director is charged with.

In order to successfully achieve all of the above, IT Directors will need to wear a number of hats at different times. Some of the key aspects of their personality which should completely shine through are those which I outline next.

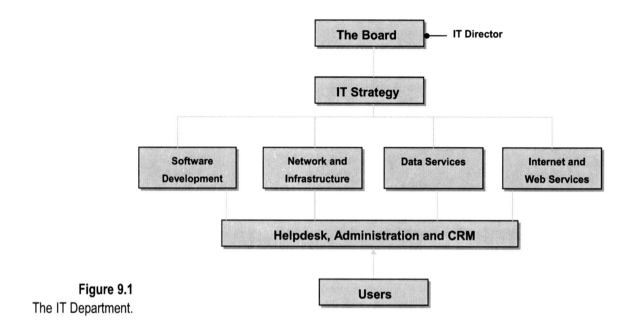

Figure 9.1
The IT Department.

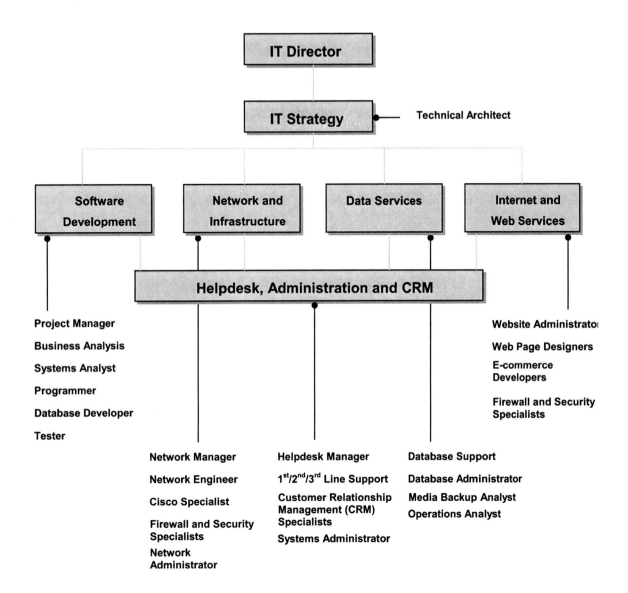

Figure 9.2
The IT Roles.

The Decision Maker

The IT Director is the person responsible for ensuring that the company's IT investments are aligned with the company's strategic business objectives. This means that in most organizations the IT Director does much of the long-term thinking and lays down policies relating to nearly all areas of IT. The instigators of change, their decisions will ultimately impact the organisations choice of network architecture, desktop applications, database architecture, software development tools, web strategy, IT vendors, IT support and even the layout of the IT helpdesk.

Since all of these activities are now such an integral part of today's business model, it's not difficult to see how stressful this role can often become. A number of IT departments are constantly tugging at the IT Director's ear at any one time, imploring them for a slice of the company's IT budget. However, regardless of the size of company, the IT budget is a finite (and always inadequate) amount, and in the long run really serves only one purpose; to realize key business aims.

As a result experienced IT Directors are never surprised to find themselves operating in a highly political environment, so a thick skin is absolutely essential in this role as is the ability to say 'No' without offending.

The Inquisitor

IT Directors are the ultimate inquisitors. They need to have a number of questions clearly answered before they can compile a strategy for change. Questions such as;

•   What is this company's mission or purpose?

•   What is this company's strategic three to five year plan?

•   How does technology fit into the business goals?

•   What are the most important things that IT needs to focus on to support the company's business goals?

- What are the company's greatest business and IT challenges?

- What level of human resources do I need in place?

- What sort of partnerships and alliances do we need to establish?

- Do we outsource IT or keep it in-house?

What We Should See on Their CVs

Key Skills and Characteristics

Below are some required character traits of an IT Director in more detail:

Strong business skills

As we've already established, the duties of today's IT Director require a variety of skill sets which include considerable business prowess, strong leadership qualities and core technical awareness. Their CV should be a descriptive record of how they mapped IT initiatives towards business goals, and should exude evidence of their finesse in using pivotal IT technologies in today's business environment.

High level of education

IT directors will generally be highly educated in a technical discipline, though exceptions to this can be found. As well as having acquired substantial experience in their chosen industry sector, they will most likely have a technical (if not computer science) degree as well as further computing accreditations picked up during their expeditions through the various companies in which they have worked. However, an IT Director will never be required to roll up their shirt sleeves and jump in with the programmers when resources are scarce.

Diplomacy and leadership

So whereas traditionally a very technical background was crucial for this role, in today's highly charged corporate environment the position has transformed into a somewhat more business oriented function and is often much less technically hands on. A strong sense of self-assurance, diplomacy and leadership are just as valued a commodity as a strong core technical expertise.

Delegation and facilitation

In actual fact many of today's large corporations don't want to see IT Directors behaving as technical experts, rather as business executives who can swiftly channel the talents of dedicated technical advisors; i.e. the technical architects and lead programmers hired specifically for this purpose. They should possess the ability to delegate, or facilitate and coach where necessary. Instrumental in this role is also the ability to foresee and resolve potential and actual conflicts between department and individuals at various levels in the organization. Finally your typical IT Director will write report after report outlining all of their thoughts and actions, and therefore superb written and oral communication skills are a must.

Presentation and debating

As a key part of the role involves trying to influence people both within and outside of the organization, it is imperative that an IT Director be able to put together reports and proposals, and be able to present their ideas with clarity to all sizes of audience; from a small boardroom meeting to an AGM company conference.

Which other roles do IT Directors influence

Of course, in some form or other, this very senior role influences all of the IT roles below them. However there are certain roles that exist primarily to help serve the ultimate purpose of the IT Director. These include;

Technical Architect

(This role is covered in considerable detail in Chapter 11).

Briefly, a Technical Architect is the most senior of the hands-on IT technical roles. They have a formidable understanding of IT across the board (application software, network architecture, operating systems etc.) yet with all of their vast experience they have chosen to focus on reaching even greater heights as a technical expert and a lead figure for the IT department; rather then making that move across to people management, project management or even IT Directorship. They love all of the challenges associated with a rapidly evolving IT infrastructure and as a result are indispensable to an IT Director for the advice and technical guidance which they can offer.

Business Analyst

(This role is covered in more detail in Chapter 12.)

A surprising person you might think to be associated with the IT Director. After all Business Analysts (BA) generally aren't technical gurus, and are brought on at the very early stages of a new project because of their understanding of the business. Their key purpose in life is to speak to users, and to ensure that the needs of the user are suitably gathered, documented and passed on to the real techies who can then start to convert these findings into a useful IT tool. However, in many ways a BA acts as a type of safety mechanism for senior roles such as the IT Director. Remember that an IT Director is not free from blame or accountability. On the contrary financial accountability rests with them. They ultimately need to justify their decisions to the CEO, to the board and to the shareholders of that company. And when things go awry, they need to be able to explain why they went down a particular decision-making route. In this situation the IT Director can always turn to the findings of the BA, citing that it was only after the results of the extensive feasibility study that such a decision was made.

Programme and Project Manager

(These roles are covered in more detail in Chapter 10.)

It goes without saying that all of the senior roles associated with key projects are in constant communication with the IT Director. Programme Managers are effectively the project managers of multiple projects. They oversee a number of projects, which are often linked at higher level by a key business purpose as outlined by the IT Director.

Key Tools, Technologies and Concepts Associated with this Role

Besides everything mentioned so far, here are additional concepts, technologies and tools which you need to look out for when studying the CV of an IT Director.

Systems Design and Planning

As was mentioned previously, in strict terms this is no longer the realm of the IT Director. A technical architect will nearly always be the person who gets down to the hands-on design of a new system (see page 166 for more detail as to how this is done). However, an IT Director will need to be comfortable and up to speed with the key strengths and weaknesses of different IT systems in the market. Without this they won't be suitably equipped to influence the IT strategy in a decisive way. Generally, and primarily for a quiet life, IT Directors prefer **homogenous** systems and try and steer clear of any leanings towards **heterogeneous** architecture (if you're unclear about these, see page 162 for an explanation of these terms).

Systems Integration

Mergers or alliances between companies may sound like a superb strategic move to a company CEO and their board, but these can often pose an immense challenge from an IT perspective. In fact, there have been occasions where a merger has looked great on paper only to be called off at the last minute because of the seemingly insurmountable challenges linked to making the IT systems merge. As a result IT Directors will nearly always be required to have had exposure to situations where a *systems integration* project was carried out, either due to a company or department merger. Systems integration is needed when different IT technologies of any sort need to come together to work seamlessly. Once again Technical Architects come to the rescue because this is their particular forte. TAs love a systems integration challenge, and they will be the first person to offer a down-to-earth sober appraisal as to how realistic the proposed *IT fusion* venture may be.

(Read much more about systems integration on page 166.)

Middleware

Nearly always, when you're trying to get disparate systems to talk to each other as with *systems integration*, you need *middleware*. Middleware is the collective name for any type of intelligent software which enables different systems to talk to each other – i.e. different application software, different networks, different operating systems etc. The likes of COM/DCOM, CORBA fall into this category. This is tricky, complex stuff – and so by definition falls into the realms of the TA once again. However, and just by implication, IT Directors also need to be aware of the proliferation of middleware offerings in today's IT marketplace, if only to be able to take part in meaningful discussions regarding system integration issues. They of course, leave the tricky part of using middleware to the TA.

(Middleware is explained in more detail on page 166).

Operating Systems and Platforms

Windows, Unix, DOS, MacOS. These are all operating systems, and this area of IT forms the backdrop for most of the significant battles linked with today's IT giants *viz.* Bill Gates, Steve Jobs, and Linus Torvalds (he of the Linux yarn). Operating systems are yet another area which the IT Director will need to be aware of, in order to make sound decisions. This whole area is clearly laid out for you in Chapter 4.

Business Intelligence

One of the key commodities in business today is of course **data**. Ironically, one of the biggest problems for most large companies today is that there is simply too much data flying around the organization for them to actually make any real sense of it. Data properly treated becomes information, information carefully analysed becomes knowledge, and knowledge properly acted upon becomes a distinct business advantage. But, it is a long and tedious process that ferments lifeless raw data into a pulsating piece of key knowledge. Data about your customers, data about your competitors, data about your market. It's all there, in the billion binary-coded 'zeros and ones' residing in the IT system. From the hit counter on the company web site, to the customer survey forms sitting in the company database. The art of making sense of so much data is **Business Intelligence (BI)**, and IT Directors must have an understanding of the tools and techniques available to create a clear picture of that data. These technologies include OLAP, GIS, DSS and CRM. (Read more about this in the 'Recruiting Database Specialists' section of this book in Chapter 19.)

IT Auditing and Compliance

When an IT Director wants to carry out a review of how the IT organization is supporting the company's business objectives, they carry out what is called an *IT audit*. This is usually triggered because either too many IT projects have started to fail, the IT department has started to lose credibility with key business areas, or IT investment wisdom is being questioned by areas of the business.

Some key components of an IT audit:

* The business objectives are clearly re-defined for IT.

* The IT department's structure is reviewed.

* The technology (hardware/software) is assessed.

* Staffing levels are reviewed.

* Business applications are re-assessed.

* A Findings & Recommendations report is written.

An IT audit allows a company to redefine where the focus of IT investment must be in order for IT to become a strategic aid to the business. Projects are prioritised to support business goals, and less useful projects are put on hold or terminated.

Project and Development Methodologies

Where would the world be without structured, proven ways of doing things? Documented techniques that have proven useful are passed from one generation to the next. It's the same in IT. *Methodologies* are proven successful structured ways of working within IT. There are two types of methodologies.

Project management methodologies such as PRINCE2 exist primarily to bring projects through to successful completion (more on project management methodologies on page 149). Whereas software development methodologies such as SSADM and AGILE are geared towards showing programmers how to use developing software more efficiently (read more about development methodologies in Chapter 13).

Collaboration

In essence, we use this term in the same way as you would use it in general conversation. I.e. working together towards a common goal. However, in IT, *collaboration* is using software tools, management techniques and business processes to allow different groups of people to work together more effectively. So an IT Director's role is to improve the collaboration capability between different organizations, teams, departments and individuals.

Consultancy and Outsourcing

IBM, **EDS**, **Logica**, **Cap Gemini** and **Accenture** are all IT consultancies (also known as outsourcing companies and IT Services organisations). These are companies, which when contracted, come into a business and take full responsibility for an entire IT project from start to finish. This could be anything from large-scale systems integrations project to a completely new network installation. The sums involved are often huge, and so their clients are usually very large, profitable organizations such as pharmaceuticals, investment banks, government departments or airlines. An example of the sheer scale of projects as taken on by consultancies is that of EDS who designed and implemented the **Naval Marine Corps Intranet** (otherwise known as the **NMCI**). Such a project cost the client, the US navy, around $9billion dollars and resulted in possibly the largest private network in the world with some 400,000 users capable of using the system at any one time. IT Directors who stem from a consultancy background will typically have tackled a wide spectrum of technical challenges linked to business strategy, which bodes very well for their new employer.

Compliance

New rules and regulations arise every day in relation to company law and financial accountability. *Compliance* is the act of ensuring that you are aware of these regulations and are adhering to them. Much of the responsibility relating to compliance issues falls upon the IT Director. However this area has become such a high-profile issue in recent times (especially in response to the fraudulent activities and financial scandals following the collapse of Enron and WorldCom) that Chief Compliance Officers (CCOs) are now enlisted solely to take care of such matters and to ensure that shareholders and employees are protected under similar circumstances. In the United States the **Sarbanes-Oxley Act (SOx)** was passed to restore investor confidence after the Enron fiasco to underwrite the integrity of financial information. UK companies with a presence in the US are also subject to the act and many believe that the UK will follow suit across the board.

Corporate Governance

This can be defined broadly as the relationship of a company to its employees, shareholders, financial bodies, and even society as a whole. Governance is about promoting corporate fairness, transparency and accountability to all of these parties; and so this concept goes hand-in-hand with compliance.

Interim Management

Occasionally you will be privileged enough to meet the rare creature who takes the form of a **contract IT Director**, known as an **Interim Manager**. There is usually only one reason for taking on these very expensive, very sinister consultants. And that is to purge the company of all that is wasteful and unnecessary – even if that means rivers of blood flowing through your organization. Interims usually mean drastic change. Streamlining, restructuring – call it what you will. Entire departments could be decimated in their wake, but they *do* get the company back on track. A tongue-in-cheek term that is sometimes applied to this role is '**Seagull Management**', i.e. someone who flies in from out of nowhere, craps on you from a great height, and then disappears never to be seen again!

Hint: By the way, don't use the term 'seagull management' when interviewing interims – they really don't like to hear it!

Interviewing IT Directors

When interviewing an IT Director you should simply try to gather as many examples as you possibly can in relation to all of the above skills and traits (i.e. instances which highlight their business skills, leadership, conflict resolution capabilities etc). As a little footnote here, don't feel too phased or concerned that you are asking questions that might appear to be elementary or even too quizzical of a person of such obvious position and gravitas (you might also feel this reticence when interviewing other senior roles such as a technical architect). Remember, there is a professional business transaction going on in any interview situation – your role as the interviewer is to accumulate as much information as you possibly can in order to market this person properly, and the interviewee's duty here is to allow you to do this in as efficient a way as possible.

Remember to start jotting down situations that show their familiarity with some of the above strategic areas such as:

•   Corporate governance.

•   Data mining and business intelligence.

•   Auditing.

•   Project and development Methodologies.

•   Consultancy.

•   Outsourcing (BPO).

•   Compliance.

Summary

So there it is. Generally the highest-ranking role in IT, defined in a way that will (hopefully) help you in an interview situation. I hope from what's been said you're beginning to appreciate why these people are revered as they are. These are exciting times for corporate IT, but it is left to the IT Director to strike that delicate balance between going overboard in the use new technology and experimenting with new IT concepts to achieve business nirvana.

> # And finally – The Age Old Truisms of IT Directorship
>
> - By the time you've read about a technology, it's no longer a strategic advantage.
>
> - Users don't understand IT – never have, never will. All they really understand is their jobs.
>
> - The most powerful influence on CEOs' IT preferences are the people who write for airline in-flight magazines.
>
> - Faster hardware won't solve your business problems … unless your business problem is slow hardware.
>
> - Functionality isn't the same as usefulness.
>
> - When you just have a hammer, everything looks like a nail. Most IT people just have technology.
>
> - The systems that last are the ones you were counting on to be obsolete.
>
> - Old ideas got that way because they proved useful.
>
> - Fast – Good – Cheap. . . . .Pick any two!

CHAPTER TEN

Recruiting Project Managers

Introduction

I feel sorry for my mate Imran. I've known him since we were both in our teens, and to this day he remains one of my dearest friends. It was always taken as read that (much like the rest of us lads) he was a decent, amiable bloke who enjoyed the usual things associated with being a student (football, pizzas, not studying, movies, girls etc.).

But more than all of us, Imi liked a quite life. His digs at university weren't always completely tidy (often resembling the aftermath of a bad summer at Glastonbury) but then whose were? The back of his 1985 Vauxhall Chevette sometimes harboured the odd box of half-eaten pizza and the occasional empty coke can. **And then he ended up marrying Ruby.**

"Some people have accused me of micromanaging!
Do you agree with them? If so, say yes."

As you progress in IT recruitment and start to interview more and more candidates, one thing will become glaringly obvious. That there are some roles in IT which intrinsically take over the very core of a person. Either this, or the person was simply *born* to do that role in the first place. Having programmed in Fortran and Finite Element Analysis for two years during my Mechanical/Aeronautical Engineering degree, I'm convinced that programmers (the really good programmers) are genetically hard-wired in a certain way to enjoy this stuff. Similarly, you should be able to spot a really good Project Manager (PM) from a mile off. Everything they do, and the way they do it screams

"I exist to bring order and harmony to every aspect, every activity within my life, and whilst I'm at it the lives of all with whom I interact. Behold, I am PM, the destroyer of entropy, the nemesis of chaos."

We all love Ruby dearly. But Ruby is an IT project manager for one of the leading investment banks in the City, and a very good one at that. And every activity that goes on in Imran's house, from arranging the summer holidays, to shopping for Imran's underwear; from taking the kids to the cinema, to organising a barbeque, is meticulously planned and executed. All elements of risk are analysed, and minimised. Their house move was choreographed via Microsoft Project (which still didn't prevent Imran snapping the top off of their giant rubber tree plant). Ruby is an excellent project manager because **it is at the very core of her being**.

Imran is now an organised, smart and disciplined individual. He no longer remains the same person we knew at Uni.

On a personal note, I know that you will be reading this Imran and this is just to let you know, from the rest of the lads and myself, that *we all feel for you man – keep the faith!*

Before the Project

The BA has come and gone. The feasibility study is over and the results are in. There is an eerie sort of silence that has engulfed the trade floor now. The mumblings of discontent over the dilapidated old IT software have now abated. There is now a new rumour making its way around the company. It appears that the project to develop the new system might actually go ahead!

Prior to any project kicking off however a number of steps have to be taken. The first of these is for all the parties who will be involved in the new system and its development (the '**system stakeholders**') to agree what the system should be required to do and approximately when it should be completed. The outcome of these initial discussions is documented in what is often called the **Project Initiation Document** (**PID**). This is then developed further into a more detailed '**statement of work**' or 'Terms of Reference' for the project which is explained below.

Terms of Reference

The '**Terms of Reference**' (**TOR**) sets out in more detail the framework for the new project including its scope and goals. This document must always be agreed upon before any serious work on the project can begin.

The TOR is usually set out by one or more of the following:

*   IT Director.

*   A Systems Steering Committee.

*   The project sponsor.

*   Senior Systems Analyst or Business Analyst.

And so to the Project

So what exactly is an IT project? A project is a collection of linked activities with a clearly defined start and finishing point. It should result in the delivery of an effective solution delivered to the required standards within a predefined timescale and within certain cost restraints. A very tall order indeed.

Rarely do organisations achieve all of above in their IT projects. Sometimes the required standards are met but at the cost of time, sometimes the project comes in on time but is way over budget. The extent to which all of these objectives are met is primarily down to the talents of the Project Manager. So this is a role with immense responsibilities.

In his book *The Handbook of Project Management* Trevor Young defines a project as follows:

A project;

- has a **specific purpose** which can be readily defined,

- is **unique**, because it is most unlikely to be repeated in exactly the same way by the same group of people to give the same results,

- is **focused on the customer** and customer expectations,

- is **not usually routine** work but may contain some routine-type tasks,

- is made up of a **series of activities** that are linked together, all contributing to the desired result,

- has clearly defined **time constraints** – a date when the results are required,

- is frequently **complex** because the work may involve people in different departments, and even on different sites, and

*   has **cost constraints** which must be clearly defined and understood to ensure that the project remains viable.

The Project Manager Mindset

Recently, after a week of training around Europe, I found myself sitting in yet another airport lounge contemplating whether or not to open up the laptop and get cracking and feed more material into 'The *infernal* Guide' (that's what this book was occasionally known as when frustration set in); or, to simply forget it, chill out, and wait for the gate number to appear on the screen. I was fatigued after numerous consecutive days of training and at this point 'The Guide' did NOT seem '*full of supportive love and wisdom*'; in fact at times like these The Guide was becoming '*a never-ending pain*' and I really wasn't in the mood to get back to structuring chapters once more. However the message that then appeared on the airline display screen soon made my decision for me. The flight back to London was going to be delayed by a further two hours and we wouldn't be arriving at Stansted until 1.00 am at the earliest. Under my breath I joined the chorus of groans that emanated from the lounge. I had then just about made up my mind to go off, buy a completely non-IT-related magazine, and head to the nearest coffee bar. However, my eyes fell upon a petite Korean lady sitting next to me. Though ordinary and unassuming, she had just unzipped a large leather holdall. She slid off from her chair, knelt down on the carpet and started to pull out its contents and lay them about her neatly. I was intrigued. She soon had her mp3 player plugged into her ears and was humming away, and unperturbed by the goings on around her, then proceeded to unravel three large scrolls of paper which when joined together formed a continuous chart full of complex schematic drawings and descriptions in the tiniest font size. The lady was an IT project manager and this chart was a timeline of how her project was proceeding. It had the names of every individual involved, the tasks to be done and the milestones which needed to be met. She then happily started to hum and scribble away with a pencil. Adjust, rub out, and scribble once more. And I watched in awe.

Inspired, it didn't take me long to grab a quick take-away coffee and come back.

I sat next to her, opened up my laptop and poured out almost a complete chapter for *The Beloved Guide*.

That's what these people are about. Even if they are overseeing a team of two hundred individuals, each with their own numerous and assorted duties, PMs can somehow sleep soundly at night. This is because they have learned to think in a modular, compartmentalised way. They are able to sort their project risks into four key areas as shown below:

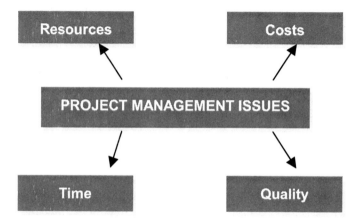

In more detail, these are:

Time – not just in terms of time taken to complete the project, but also the **opportunity cost** relating to time which could potentially be better spent in other projects or pursuits.

Costs – as outlined in the budget for the project.

Resources – including human resources, machinery, space etc.

Quality – in terms of the standards of quality initially agreed upon.

Let's look at this role in detail.

The Role In Detail

Key Responsibilities

A project manager is first and foremost a leader and so must display the standard set of leadership qualities that satisfy three overlapping sets of needs as shown in the diagram below:

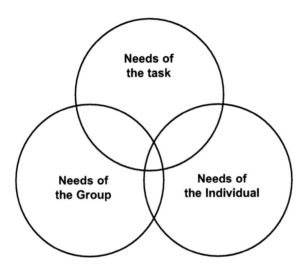

They need to be expert in dividing their time and their focus in the above three areas; whilst all the time having the final objective in mind. The following are key responsibilities for the PM.

Establishing Leadership and Team Structure

In order to ensure that all the above discrete groups are adequately controlled, they break down the challenge as follows:

Needs of the task include
*   Defining tasks.

*   Planning work.

- Allocating resources.

- Assigning responsibilities.

- Monitoring progress.

- Checking performance.

- Controlling quality.

Needs of the group include:
- Building and maintaining team spirit.

- Setting standards and maintaining discipline.

- Setting up systems for team communication.

- Training the team.

- Appointing team leaders.

Needs of the individual include:
- Developing the individual.

- Balancing group and individual needs.

- Rewarding good performance.

- Helping with personal problems.

The Structure of Project Teams

The PM will need to organise project teams each of which can fall into the following categories:

Specialist teams

Typically, specialist project teams within a project may consist of individuals selected from the following groups:

• Specialist IT staff (systems analysts, programmers etc.).

• Specialist functional staff (contributing technical and business process advice).

• User representatives (who will be monitoring the systems response to live data and real-market conditions).

• Human resource development and training specialist.

• External consultants (who can bring in specialist technical or functional expertise).

Each of these teams will have an appointed team leader responsible for;

• Planning and organising the work of the team members on a weekly basis.

• Supervising the activity of individuals.

• Coordinating intercommunication between teams and departments.

• Reporting to and conferring with the project manager on an on-going basis.

• Reporting back to the team members all relevant developments.

Other specialist teams include:

The User Group

In most large projects it is a prudent measure to build a structured User Group. This group will normally consist of at least one user from each of the departments affected by the project, and is an ideal forum for business-oriented end users to be involved in the technical development of the new system. This is an ideal forum for users to express their concerns and give feedback as the system develops.

The Project Steering Committee

This committee has the responsibility of overseeing the high-level development of the system. It is this body which has one eye on the overall strategic IS (Information Systems) strategy of the company and so is ideally placed to make key decisions relating to how *this* particular project impacts that strategy. This committee will be made up of senior representatives from the IS team, the business sections, and the financial management teams, and as a result has the power to recommend that projects and recommendations are actioned. They decide which projects take priority and which ones should be put on hold or scrapped all together.

So What Is a Programme Manager?

Before we move on it's worth mentioning that a **programme manager** is someone who is often perceived to have more seniority than a project manager. And rightly so. Programme Managers are projects managers of multiple projects. They will have many project managers reporting in to them on a daily basis, all of whom are focused on delivering one giant end result through the combined effects of their individual projects. Programme Managers are generally thinking at a higher strategic level (almost on par with the IT Director) and of course control much larger budgets than usual. But, very often, they still use many of the basic tools utilised by project managers (such as PM software, Gantt charts etc.) to monitor how each project is advancing.

What We Should See on Their CVs

Key Skills and Characteristics

So from everything we have said so far about PMs, their core skills and characteristics must revolve around:

Leadership
A project manager must be able to stimulate action, progress and change.

Technological understanding
A project manager needs to have an accurate perception of the technical requirements of the project so that business needs are addressed and satisfied.

Evaluation and decision-making
A project manager should have the ability to evaluate alternatives and make informed decisions.

People management
A project manager must be able to motivate and enthuse their teams and have a personal drive towards achieving project goals.

Planning and control
A project manager should be able to constantly monitor progress against the plan and take any necessary corrective action using structured monitoring methods.

Financial Awareness
A project manager should be proficient in financial risk management and have a broad financial knowledge.

Procurement
A project manager should be able to develop the basic procurement strategy for the project.

Communication

A project manager should be able to express themselves in a clear and unambiguous manner both orally and written with a wide range of people.

Legal and Contractual

A project manager should have an awareness of the legal issues that might affect a project and be comfortable with the contracts which define the project, and the relationship with subcontractors.

Risk Management

A project manager should always be adept at risk management because all projects are susceptible to some elements of risk. This could include cost overrun, missed deadlines, poor outcome, disappointed customers, and business disruption. Risk management is the identification and handling of risks in a way that will minimise disruption to the project.

Tools, Technologies and Concepts Associated with this Role

PRINCE2 and Other Project Management Methodologies

As mentioned previously in The Guide, **methodologies** are defined as proven, structured ways of working. In IT there are two types of methodologies, and many new recruiters are unclear as to the distinction between the two.

- **Project management methodologies** exist primarily to bring projects through to successful completion (relevant to this role). However,

- **Software development methodologies** such as **SSADM** and **AGILE** are geared towards simply towards showing programmers how to use development languages more efficiently (and have nothing specifically to do with this role but are thoroughly discussed in the software development part of this guide in Chapter 7).

A project management methodology aims to ensure that all of the key issues which need to be addressed within a project are properly monitored. It also lays out a number of health checks along the way so that it is easier for the PM to recognise when elements of the project might be starting to slide or go off the rails.

Most project managers will use a methodology of some description to help them bring a project through to completion. It could even be a methodology which they have created and perfected themselves. There are many methodologies developed by people around the world based on their own experiences within projects, however in the UK one of the most popular methodologies is **PRINCE2** which stands for (**Pr**ojects **IN C**ontrolled **E**nvironments) and is a methodology developed for and championed by the UK government. PRINCE2 lays down structure through focusing on eight key components of management (although there are 45 sub-processes within the methodology).

The eight components or PRINCE2 are:

- **Defining the Business Case** – Ensuring that the project is justified.

- **Organisation** – Roles are put into place from Programme Manager downwards.

- **Producing Product Plans and Flow diagrams** – Documentation to show what should be achieved at each stage of the project and who is responsible for each stage.

- **Control Management** – Exception management, control bands and highlight reports are all ways to ensure that the project is controlled affectively.

- **Risk Management** – Monitoring the risk to the project and the business at any stage.

- **Quality Management** – Adhering to set levels of quality so that the end product conforms to standards.

- **Configuration Management** – Version control of products and tools within the project.

- **Change Management** – Monitoring if circumstantial changes within or outside the project have an impact on the outcome.

The world's largest project management professional body is the **Project Management Institute** (**PMI**), and has examination centres throughout the world. They have a certification examination leading to the **Project Management Professional** (**PMP**) qualification. There are numerous other methodologies besides those mentioned above including the popular **Six Sigma** which was developed by Motorola as a methodology to ensure quality and minimise defects in any process.

Different PM Methodologies for Different Approaches to Development

Many methodologies, such as PRINCE2, are structured and work hand in hand with the waterfall approach to development (see Chapter 7 for a complete explanation of this); however there are some PM methodologies, such as **Scrum,** which are designed to work specifically with **iterative** and **RAD** based approaches to development such as **AGILE** (see Chapter 8 for a complete explanation of this).

More Project Management Tools

Besides methodologies, a project manager has a range of software tools available to assist with planning and control; and these have been refined and developed over the years but are all designed to improve the effectiveness of the project management process.

Project management tools include:

*   Work Breakdown Structure.

*   Gantt chart.

*   Open Workbench (Open Source).

*   MS Project (Microsoft).

*   KPlato (Open Source).

*   OmniPlan (Omni Group).

There are many more PM tools available, far too numerous to mention here. But from the above, a notable concept is the **Gantt chart**. Attributed to Henry Gantt, this was originally drawn on a single large sheet of paper to represent the phases and activities of a project in detail. All of the software above will have the in-built capabilities to generate a Gantt chart.

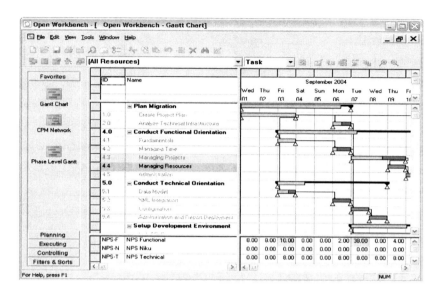

Figure 10.1
A Gantt chart
generated from Open
Workbench
(Courtesy: Open
Source Community).

PM software of course makes it far easier for a project manager to delve into
any aspect of the project by bringing the Gantt chart to life and making it multi-
dimensional. So a simple click of a button within Open Workbench reveals all
the detail they need, as shown below:

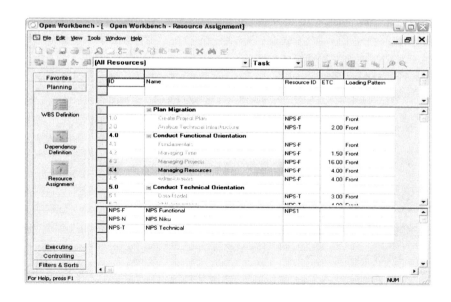

Figure 10.2
A Resource
Assignment table
generated from Open
Workbench
(Courtesy: Open
Source Community).

My inspirational lady in the airport lounge in Zurich; she was simply reviewing
her Gantt chart!

Interviewing Project Managers

Collating all of the ideas which we've discussed in this chapter; here are some key reminders to prepare you for an interview with a project management candidate:

Look through the past roles on their CVs and check as to the size of budgets mentioned. Very often these are 'rounded up,' or do not reflect the reality of how much of the budget was actually directly held by your candidate and his or her team. Ask them how much of the budget they themselves had direct control of.

Similarly, get an accurate view of the size of the teams which this candidate had direct control over. Ask how the teams were divided (i.e. did this PM have control over a Project Steering Committee and other specialist teams etc.) Numerous specialist teams and user groups implies a much more complex project than a single large team.

Ask about their views on methodologies mentioned on their CV, and the strengths and weaknesses of each. Have they had to tune and customise these for certain projects.

Ask about their experiences within projects when things didn't go exactly to plan (no project is without its drama). What was their course of action in the event of unforeseen situations?

Check how they got to the PM stage of their life. Was it through a technical path (i.e. from a fledgling programmer, engineer etc.), or did they come through the business analyst stream (in which case they may be perceived as being slightly less technical). If they are not overly technical ask them how they have dealt with situations where they have had to maintain credibility around technical experts and hands-on techies.

Summary

What a wonderful role to recruit for. These are generally mature, stable individuals who were born to tackle pressure and responsibility. I know from experience that they tend to be amiable and presentable from the outset (not implying, of course, that others within IT aren't!). They'll usually be happy to have detailed discussions with you about their past, as the art of speaking to people and presenting themselves is part and parcel of their day-to-day existence. So you'll spend less time worrying about how they'll behave in the interview, and whether or not they actually bothered to turn up well presented.

And finally, if they do get the job, you will hopefully have made a lasting friendship with someone who spends most of their time hiring many IT roles for a myriad of different projects!

CHAPTER ELEVEN

Recruiting Technical Architects

Introduction

"Mr. Hunt, this isn't mission 'difficult',
it's mission impossible.
'Difficult' should be a walk in the park for you."

Mission Commander Swanbeck.
Mission Impossible II

So you've received yet *another* top-ranking role to work on. Well done, this is a great role to recruit, but be prepared to bow and/or curtsy. Technical Architects are considered to be the intellectual giants of IT. These are the renaissance men and women of technology. They can make an IT system *sing*, when previously it was beginning to groan! They are often revered in the organizations in which they find themselves – and why not. IT at this level is no longer about following procedures and repeating the tried and tested practices of the past. These people come on board because the tried and tested approach simply won't work any more. When we need to get creative with IT, when we have wandered unsteadily into a new and uncharted IT terrain, we look for a TA to help us get out. Whereas most IT roles are about making IT work properly, TAs are much more about being innovative with IT; be it in relation to software, hardware or infrastructure problems. Constantly pushing IT to new levels, these are the individuals who *will* find a way to overcome the immense technical hurdles which arise in today's demanding corporate IT environment. If you need the answer to a tortuous IT conundrum, or if parts of your IT system are starting to wobble unsteadily, refusing to talk to each, or failing to share data smoothly, you need a TA.

But, how will you know?

So, as a mere mortal how will you know you're in the presence of a true Technical Architect? Well it's relatively simple. You'll be able to spot a bone-fide TA immediately because of the following telltale signs:

1.   They often hover and float across the office floor, rather then walk.

2.   Their frontal lobes occasionally resemble those of the characters from the Tefal adverts of the seventies (younger readers may need to research this a bit – just Google it).

3.   Their general demeanour is that of the condescending yet polite aliens from a far superior civilization as depicted in the sci-fi movies of the late 1950s. You know the ones, they arrive on Earth in the form of blonde people with immensely large foreheads, and dressed like keen amateur golfers. The key differences being that TA's aren't necessarily blonde, not always polite and generally have a poorer dress sense...

Enough jesting … let's take a closer look at this role.

"I introduced the world's first
nose-top computer 18 months ago.
Sales are slower than originally anticipated."

The Role in Detail

The TA in the Project Lifecycle

That was a huge build up, so let's come back down to earth and get to know some of the key aspects of this role. Firstly, let's remind ourselves at which stage the TA makes an appearance in the project lifecycle, and the questions they usually need to ask:

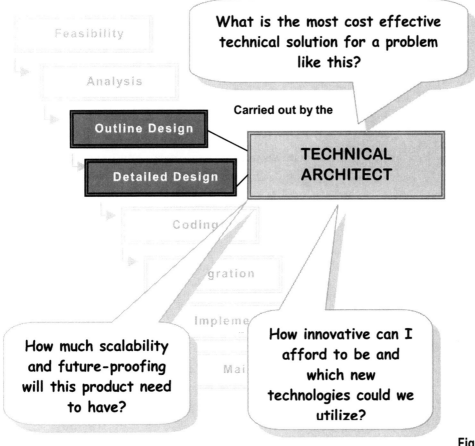

Figure 11.1
The Technical
Architect in the
Project Lifecycle.

The Key Responsibilities of a TA

Also referred to as the **Lead Architect**, **Technical Authority**, **Technical Lead**, or **Senior Applications Designer**; a Technical Architect (TA) is the person who everyone turns to (including the IT Director) for greater wisdom in technical matters. Specifically, they carry out a number of key functions which include:

•   Acting as an advisor to the IT director in all matters relating to the IT strategy of the company.

•   Designing solutions to meet the technical problems of the project.

•   Acting as a technical lead, advisor and mentor to programmers, network engineers and other hands on staff (depending on the nature of the project).

•   Daring to be the IT visionary, with an eye on all the leading edge IT stuff which could have an impact on the project and its success.

Buyer Beware – There are Architects and There are *Architects*

A friend of mine owns race horses (or to be precise – *a race horse*). Though it's never been a huge life-long ambition of mine to own one of these beautiful creatures, she did once proffer some advice which, it occurs to me, has a little to do with the topic in discussion. "If you ever think of investing in one…" she said, "make sure you never buy one that goes by the name of 'Thunderbolt' or 'Hell Raiser'."

"Ahaah." I said enthusiastically, thinking I had completely grasped her point. *"Because these are the out-of-control nutters who you'll never be able to tame!"*

"No!" She sighed disappointedly. "Because they're the ones who are either on the mend from a really bad injury, or who'll never make it around the track because of chronic arthritis! They are given the exotic names to lure some poor unknowing sap into thinking they've landed a real power-house of an animal!"

And there ended, once and for all, my brief forray into the world of racehorses.

In the same vain, you'll find that the term 'architect' is often over-used in IT. Both clients and candidates will partake in a quick round of 'trip up the recruiter' when they feel it is necessary to do so. Call me a cynic, but once again I speak from personal experience in terms of handling such roles.

Your clients will occasionally (in a futile attempt to repackage and over-sell a less glamorous role) enhance the job's chances of being spotted, by adorning the role with the glowing title of 'Architect'. Conversely, any eager candidate focused on trying to make that quick leap into the *serious money*, from their last few roles as 'potentially a better then average programmer', will think about re-branding themselves as a TA; knowing that the very mention of the word 'architect' on a CV can make a fledgling recruiter go weak at the knees. It takes a lot of practice to differentiate the true TAs from those who are staking their claim to this prized status simply because they've been around for ages.

Just to make the whole picture slightly more confusing, the term 'architect' is often used in order to describe those who are considered to be experts in a particular area; such as **Network Architect, Applications Architect, Systems Architect, Web Architect** and **Software Architect.** And undoubtedly you'll see many of these alternatives cropping up on CVs and job specs. As a rule these are all variations to the theme of TA, and can generally be considered (though not always) to be niche versions of the architect role.

What I mean by this last point is that truly seasoned Technical Architects will have had exposure to solving the technical issues relating to the 'big stuff' i.e. company mergers, implementation of new architecture from scratch which must talk to existing legacy systems (**legacy** is a term in IT that means the current, usually older, technologies within the company). For this reason I sometimes think that the term '**Solutions Architect**' is a better description (depending on the context in which you need them).

Let's take a look at the role in more detail.

What We Should See on Their CVs

Key Skills and Characteristics

The Technical Guru

Technology, technology, technology! This point is non-negotiable, simply not up for discussion. TAs will need, by definition, to have a very strong technical background. As in the case of IT Directors, they will also have had exposure to a myriad of different IT environments throughout their career. However, a TA's CV should be bursting with clear evidence of actual hands-on experience when it comes to moulding and developing a diverse range of environments and technologies too.

A wise geek (can't remember who) once reminded me that any IT system is similar to a dirt track. In the early days, when it's all brand new, the road seems smooth and fairly even; and you can drive along without too many problems. But a hundred users and managers later, all adding their own mistakes, ideas and errors eventually form dangerous grooves over time. These grooves are so intrinsic to the architecture they eventually become a part of it. The TA needs to know whether or not to keep 'shovelling' grit into the grooves, or to simply start afresh and re-surface the whole path.

The IT Director's Technical Advisor

Technical Architects must be very comfortable in taking up the role of advisor to the IT Director. In today's recruitment environment, IT Directors who stem from a heavily technical background are often hard to find. It's not that they are rare, but if a company does manage to track down this valuable commodity (or you find one for them) be assured that they must be willing to pay over the odds to procure them. Moreover, IT Directors are brought on primarily to be the individual focused on ensuring that the IT strategy is aligned with the long-term needs of the business (explained thoroughly in the chapter on Recruiting IT Directors on page 119). So when IT Directors are not the technical geniuses we would love them to be in an ideal world, they often rely heavily on their trusty Technical Architect to guide them along in their decision making process, and to help them map a solution that meets the human needs of the organisation.

Woven into the grand design of most IT Directors' strategies is the subtle yet lingering influence of a really good TA. For in reality there is no one more suited to deliver counsel on matters relating to the new 'bleeding edge' stuff that's just emerging from the research labs which might be worth looking at, or those technologies which are just over the horizon that might reward your organisation with that vital nanosecond lead over that of your rival.

However, there are often tensions in this relationship too. An IT Director is always concerned about cost and future-proofing with regards the investments that are going to be making. They are forever replaying risk analysis scenarios in their mind; whilst the TA paints vivid pictures of 'what could be' if we went with this latest thing. Technical Architects must occasionally be able to offer the most inventive solution to a problem, whilst IT Directors have to walk a fine line between accepting radical solutions and maintaining viability at a financial level. **Heterogeneous systems** (ones that have a wide diversity of different technologies, software, hardware and networks) are all very exciting, but to what extent are they a necessity for the solution? After all which end user wouldn't *want* to be issued with the latest Wi-Max enabled laptop with the latest parallel processing capability and virtual reality screen glasses – and which TA wouldn't want to be seen as the first pioneer of this technology in a business environment?

Novice TAs and users love heterogeneous systems. These are more exciting and treat each user as an individual.

Conversely, IT Directors and seasoned TAs prefer **homogenous systems**; these are boring but make economic sense. Homogenous systems are the ones in which every user has pretty much the same sort of standard hardware, each loaded with uniform software, ideally from a single vendor. Therefore the resulting solution will be more predictable and the architecture more consistent. This also means fewer companies will need to get involved in matters of support and upgrades etc. All of which ultimately has an impact on the **TCO** (total cost of ownership) per user.

The TA has to design new and innovative solutions whilst *keeping the IT Director sweet*, or risk getting a reputation in the industry for being a flamboyant over-spender of other people's money.

The Problem Solver

And so we come to the main reason why Technical Architects are famous in the industry. We hire them as IT experts with such a wide range of experiences that they can either design an enterprise wide software solution from scratch, fix what isn't working in the current network, change or upgrade the existing architecture, or to make two disparate systems work together where previously there was no need for these to communicate.

These areas are respectively coined;

- Applications Architecture Development (designing a set of applications that work together across a business).

- Systems Architecture Development. (Designing a new network architecture to work with existing business process and applications.)

- Systems Migration. (Bringing the business and its applications and data from one system over to another.)

- Systems Upgrade (upgrading a system or network to the next version and ensuring data and applications work).

- Systems Integration (making two totally different systems, business application suites or networks come together and communicate).

If you look closely at the above points once more, you'll realise how they are all (in some form or another) about making disparate IT entities work together. Either two completely different systems need to work seamlessly together, or current legacy systems need to get along with new-wave technologies.

All of the above are also examples of the way in which **business strategy can force large scale IT changes.**

For example, in the 21st century more and more TAs find themselves involved in systems integration situations as a result of mergers between large companies.

Company mergers are driven forward at the board level (or possibly on the golf course) where the CEOs of two large organisations shake hands. To them the pending merger makes absolute sense from a strategic business perspective. In fact to them the coming together of the two businesses might seem to feel something like this

Both of the businesses that are merging should benefit from coming together, and from bringing a range of different assets and skills to the table. The merger should, in principle, strengthen each company's chance of survival and strike fear into the heart of their rivals. Both parties will be able to reap the benefits of greater economies of scale, and a larger pool of new customers will be available for all. From a business perspective it all makes total sense. *Unfortunately the IT department don't quite see it like this.*

Occasionally, they see things slightly differently. In fact to anyone who is going to be involved in bringing all of the different IT systems of the two companies together it really looks more like this:

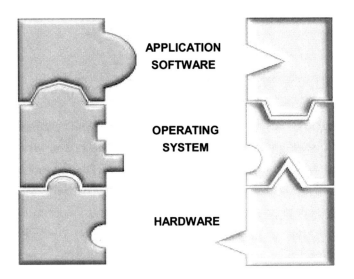

APPLICATION SOFTWARE

OPERATING SYSTEM

HARDWARE

This is what **systems integration** is really all about! And this is why we need to understand the tools which a TA would use to deal with this sort of problem. Let's do that know.

Tools, Technologies and Concepts Associated with this Role

Or *Des, Batman, The Babel Fish and Me*

As a seven year old playing outside in the back yard with my mate Desmond (gardens didn't exist in those days…just back yards); no matter where we were in our current adventure as Batman and Robin, everything would come to a grinding halt at 7.00pm every Thursday. We would dispense with our masks and cloaks, and rush inside for Aunty Lilly's fresh scones, and the latest instalment of *Star Trek* (those early expeditions led by the one true commander of the Enterprise, James. T. Kirk – none of today's modern rubbish). However, even in those halcyon days of innocence and naivety I did think it quite strange that, no matter 'how far they 'boldly went' into the galaxy, the crew of the Enterprise always found aliens that spoke perfect English; and also stumbled upon impossibly beautiful humanoid women who, of course, always fell for Kirky. Of course later on I realized that my misapprehensions were totally unfounded. We were reassured by subsequent episodes that all members of the crew were issued with **Universal Translators** (UT); devices that allowed them to understand every spoken word in the universe. An easy oversight.

As I then grew into my teens my focus was split fairly evenly between watching a rapidly-changing Samantha Chatsworth doing cartwheels in the playground, and reading science fiction in all its forms. With regards the latter I realised that this need to address the issue of translating the mutterings of alien life forms reared its head in many sci-fi movies and books. The authors couldn't ignore it. Some took the matter seriously, whilst others came up with more and more bizarre concepts of translating devices to make the storyline easier to follow. The most intriguing (tongue-in-cheek) idea of a translating device being the **Babel Fish** from the Douglas Adams novel, **The Hitchhikers Guide to the Galaxy**. The Babel Fish was an anomaly within nature. A tiny creature, which if you stuck in your ear (naturally, what else would you do with it?), would allow you to automatically decipher the brainwaves of all living things and thus enable direct translation of any galactic-language or space-dialogue which you might bump into during your pan-dimensional travels around the Universe.

Shnaar!!

Groodwaal!

Grrrrooot!

Shreek.

I say, I do like what you've done with your hair!

If you're thinking that I've just lost it at this stage, don't worry. Stay with me. Let me assure you that these aren't the ravings of a mad man. *I'm about to make a really important I.T. point here*, which is this. I, and many others from my generation, who grew up on this stuff (*Star Trek, Dr Who, Star Wars* etc.) became a part of a generation mesmerised by technology and all that it promised. These bizarre ideas inspired us if only at a subconscious level.

Samantha eventually left me for the Bay City Rollers. I grew up and pursued the whole technology theme further and made it my career. Des went on to open up a fetish dungeon in Fulham (but we should leave that story for another book). However a few from that generation, a really select few, they went on to think about this whole idea of seamless real-time *translation* more seriously. *Far more seriously.*

What I described earlier with regards the merging of two companies is a complex and challenging situation which can only be brought under control by an expert who has a particular group of skill-sets. Fundamentally, an expert who knows about *translation technologies*. This is where we need to employ the use of a TA and **middleware**.

Middleware – The Babel Fish of IT

A true, *bona fide* Technical Architect should never be afraid to deploy middleware, in fact the CV of those who claim to be seasoned TAs should always have a healthy sprinkling of middleware strewn throughout, preferably with examples of how they used it in a systems integration context. So what in reality is this *middleware*, this panacea for all technological ailments, really all about? Read on.

Middleware is a generic term for that group of software technologies which allow translation and mediation between two different systems (usually different applications) which under normal circumstances couldn't communicate. For this reason I like think of middleware as the **Babel Fish of the IT industry**. Other (less enlightened) IT analysts and techies like to refer to middleware as '**software glue**' or '**plumbing**' because it connects separate systems together. So a typical pictorial representation of middleware in any run-of-the-mill IT text book would look a little like this:

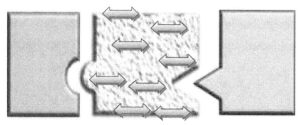

MIDDLEWARE

Though of course, any one with a bit of sense knows that there needs to be some fish in there somewhere. So my representation looks more like this:

MIDDLEWARE

Middleware technology is flexible enough to mould itself to different situations. It also has messaging capabilities which enable the translation of data between applications too. It is therefore ideally suited to applications that were originally designed to work with only one database, but which now might need to interact and share data with a range of different database systems.

As mentioned earlier, this whole area of bringing disparate systems together has been historically known as **systems integration**. However there is a more contemporary term for heterogeneous systems that have undergone the middleware treatment. When we implement such a solution across the entire business so that all of the applications now work seamlessly across the network (regardless of platform, vendor or location); this is commonly referred to as **Enterprise Application Integration** (EAI). For this reason, we often see the term **Enterprise Architect** being applied to such a role.

Examples of Middleware

There are different sub-categories of middleware (**Object-oriented middleware, Event-based middleware, Reflective middleware**), but you really don't need to understand the differences between this in the context of recruitment. You do however need to recognise the common middleware that we might see turning up on CVs. Below is a list (though not definitive any means) of middleware which you may comes across in the industry.

•   CORBA (from Object Management Group).

•   COM/DCOM (from Microsoft).

•   Websphere (from IBM).

•   Tivoli (from IBM).

•   WebLogic/ Tuxedo (from BEA).

•   Enterprise Java Beans, JNDI, JMS (from Sun, for Java).

Interviewing Technical Architects

(Whatever You Do, Don't Stroll In Unarmed!)

These men and women are paid to make the interview panel shuffle uncomfortably in their seats because the *interviewee* probably knows more then the *interviewer*, and to look down their noses at the mere MCSDs and CISCO accredited bods in the building. For this reason you, as a mere IT recruiter, must NEVER try to casually test a TA technically when they pop in to meet you. Unless you have prepared rigorously and thoroughly for this encounter (and I speak from experience), you may never recover from the mauling. After such an event, even after four weeks compassionate sick leave, you may still feel completely traumatized about the idea of returning to IT recruitment. Prepare some technical questions beforehand (ideally get a list with answers from the client) so that you are better equipped to sort out the wheat from the chaff.

Of course on the CVs of TAs we should see a range of projects that were rescued from disarray and brought into harmony using many of the technologies and concepts we have discussed above.

Ask them to explain where in their CVs the client might see evidence of the following:

- An emphasis on designing solutions; be they for infrastructure problems, development challenges or web architecture.

- Details of how they overcame key challenges within systems integration and systems planning projects.

- Exposure to technical challenges which came about as a result of corporate mergers or large scale migrations.

- An indication of the level of interaction which they had with their previous IT Directors, and to what extent they influenced IT strategy in their last few roles.

- Exposure, throughout their career, to a whole range of IT technologies; but with a focus on certain key skills geared towards the bigger problems such as the development of high-end software solutions (also in web infrastructure situations), deployment of middleware solutions, and implementing EAI and systems integration solutions.

Note: I do also want to bring to your attention to the fact that occasionally you will come across TAs who, from their CV, don't look as if they have moved around (from company to company) to the extent one might expect. This is not necessarily an indication that you don't have a skilled TA in front of you. Ask them how much **change** they have overseen. Very often staying in one place over a long period can have its benefits for too for a TA. Most TAs carry out the 'technical pruning' or creative implementations in an IT environment and then dash off to do the same elsewhere; without sticking around to study the long-term repercussions of their actions. However, those TAs who stick around for a year or so after a migration or a version change or an integration project; they are going to obtain invaluable insights into where they went wrong and how they could improve next time they come across a similar situation. So it's not always a bad thing. But, you'll need to ask, and clarify.

Summary

So there it is, the role of the Technical Architect. A tricky one to recruit for on occasions because of the wide scope which the title can encompass, and also because of the pitfalls brought about by both candidates and clients sometimes overusing the term. The added factor which a candidate-driven market (such as the one we have found ourselves in over the last few years) brings about is that your clients will want to recruit permanent TAs and pay them accordingly; whereas any candidate worth their salt will now be looking to fully exploit the market and ratchet up as many contracts as possible. But, hey! We wouldn't want the game to become too easy now would we. Happy hunting!

Interview Techniques

Interviewing Technical Architects

What we should see on their CV

- **Technical challenges being solved across a broad IT spectrum.**
  This isn't always the case (as mentioned above), but we should always see high-level problem solving preferably systems integration, systems planning and migrations.

Questions to ask

- **Get a list of technical questions (with answers) from the client.**

Skillsets and Tools

- **Middleware** (such as CORBA, DCOM, and EJB)
  Back-end Development Languages (such as Java, C++ etc.)
  Enterprise Web Development (Such as ASP.NET, XML, etc.)
  Database Connectivity (Such as JDBC)

Other

- **The should be able to demonstrate their experience in advising the IT Director in strategic IT planning and design.**

PART

5

RECRUITING THE ANALYSTS

CHAPTER TWELVE

Recruiting Business Analysts and Systems Analysts

Introduction

All change!

Developing a totally new IT system, or even modifying an existing one, is a major undertaking for any organisation. If you listen carefully enough you'll be able to hear it. In most of the corporations around the world there is (in the background) a habitual murmuring, a faintly audible underlying discontent amongst users. And their frustrations are usually aimed squarely at the IT system.

> *"It's a fantastic database, if it stayed up long*
> *enough for any of us to use it!* Or
> *"Call this a recruitment management system, I'd be better off*
> *with a pencil and some post-it notes!"*

Are amongst the lines of the well-known chorus harmonised around many of the companies I visit.

The Age Old Problem

The demand for new hardware, new software, infrastructure change; in fact any key adjustments to a company's IT make-up, is usually initiated by the moans and groans of the people on the business trade-floor (in other words you and I, the end users of that IT system). However, business users are (generally) awful when it comes to articulating themselves in an IT sense, and wouldn't know where to start in terms of properly defining their technical concerns. On the other hand,

IT experts aren't renowned for their fluency in *business-speak*. And so we have the roots of a famous impasse, which has lingered since the dawn of time (or at least the dawn of computing). For decades, people on the trade floor have continued to whine under their breath about '*that stupid computer system that never does what it's supposed to do*', without ever being able to clearly define the true cause of their anxiety.

Of course in such situations, experienced IT Directors have learned to look on tight-lipped, knowing from experience that this is probably the most prudent strategy to adopt. After all, they know that it is in the very nature of end-users to perpetually moan about their computers. IT Directors also know that evolving an IT system at any level will invariably require huge capital investment, and serious justification would be needed before such an undertaking could be initiated.

All the while, in the background, yet another guarded group of people tries its best to get on with life. The IT department. Those within this department try to ignore the side-glances of mild disdain whenever they enter the trade floor, and not feel insulted by the callous slurs that are now being directed upon their life's work. To them the IT system behaves *exactly* how it is supposed to behave … it's just that nobody was *exact* enough when we first told it how to behave!

When such chaos needs to be resolved, when we're thinking about initiating change in IT, when we need to potentially remedy the flaws in our existing set-up; the very first person we bring on board is the **Business Analyst**.

When do we need a Business Analyst?

It's a common misconception that BAs are needed only when completely new IT innovations are called for. The truth is that in today's ever-expanding corporate environment even the tiniest addition or modification to the IT system can have far-reaching strategic business implications. For this reason BAs are brought on board when almost any level of change is required. The diagram below shows the extent to which BAs get involved with change across the IT make-up of a company.

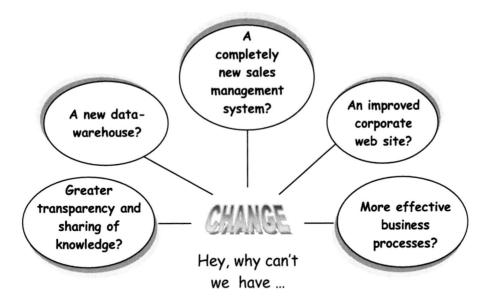

The Analyst Role in Detail

Firstly, let's remind ourselves as to when in the project lifecycle a BA makes an appearance, and the type of questions which they need answers to.

which they need answers to.

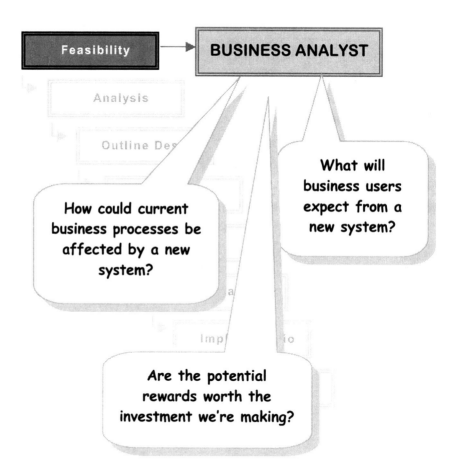

Once Again – What's in a Name?

As with many if the other IT roles, I need to once again clarify the spurious nature of the role titles used in this category. There are many areas of overlap when we consider all of the 'Analyst' roles which you might come across; and your clients may inadvertently muddy the waters even further by adding their own slant to the job description. It is important to realise that in the current IT environment there really isn't a huge difference between the roles of **Business Analyst**, and that of the **Systems Analyst**. Although there are certain skills that have historically been attributed to one or the other, the analyst roles today are so interchangeable that, in practice, there isn't much to choose between them. Most BAs can do the role of the SA and vice versa. So much so that when I'm training in continental Europe there are increasingly more and more references to the role of the '**Business Systems Analyst**' as well as '**Information Analyst**'. Both of which reinforce the idea that BA and SA are now increasingly being merged (not always, but often).

Important: The above has two implications for us as recruiters.

- **Firstly**, what I am about to impart in the rest of this chapter applies to all of the analyst roles mentioned (BA, SA or IA) – and not just to the Business Analyst role (to which I will generally make reference).

- **Secondly**, when your clients ask you to source either one of these roles, it as always worth carrying out a search on all of the above titles in your database (BA, SA, BSA and IA). Most of the candidates you speak to will have skills that are appropriate for your role, and you may be missing out on key people if you restrict your search to just BA or SA.

So let's carry on and look at some of the key aspects of the analyst role in detail.

Key Responsibilities of a Business Analyst

The Instigator of Change

The Business Analyst is the first role we see appearing on the Waterfall Model; *they trigger most large projects*. On occasions such as the one I've described in the introduction, we need someone to come along who can intervene and carry out an objective analysis of the situation. Ultimately someone who can let us know if it is actually worth ploughing substantial amounts of cash into this particular problem. This requires a combination of unique skills, as we shall find out below.

The Objective Opinion

This is a person who can speak to users in a language they understand, look at the current business processes, and tell us if the users actually have some sort of case for change (a *business case*). New software development projects, new network architectures, new hardware rollouts; they all require the nod from the BA in the first instance. Not that the BA is an extremely senior role, it isn't. But most high-ranking individuals, those who are charged with making the highest-level decisions within IT, will rely heavily on the advice and guidance of the BA.

The Insurance Policy

Bringing in a BA can also be a prudent career-saving strategy for some senior and executive roles. Think of the situation where the newly installed system actually turned out not to be such a good idea, in fact history might show that it turned out to be a disastrous decision (only noticed a few years after implementation); not only a technical failure but a move which actually resulted in an adverse affect on the overall profitability and performance of the company. This has suddenly become major deal, one that is emblazoned in newspaper headlines. Shareholders turn up to the Annual General Meetings in the form of angry mobs replete with pitchforks and torches, all baying for the IT Director's head on a stick. In such situations the hiring of a BA will have proved a very prudent safety mechanism for the IT Director, especially if the latter needs to prove that due diligence and process were adhered to in implementing the deficient system.

Evolution in IT is an expensive business. And every penny of such an investment needs to be justified by the IT Director to the board and to the company's shareholders. So before such a huge undertaking, a BA is sent in to make sure that this new and expensive IT system is actually going to be worth the headache in the long run. If it weren't for the BA, we would never have the answers needed to actually commit to change.

Key Skills and Characteristics

Below are some of the principle attributes we would normally associate with a good business/systems/analyst. As a quick overview, in general a BA must posses the following:

• Excellent communication skills, both written and oral.

• Very strong technical writing skills.

• Strong presentation skills in order to put their case across to parties at all levels.

• The ability to conduct studies and then make well-reasoned rational recommendations.

• The ability to systematically collate and evaluate data.

• A solid grasp of key areas of technology (IT architecture, relevant business software applications etc.) that could impact business processes in their industry.

• An appreciation of the current IT landscape and the in vogue technologies that could be implemented as a possible solution.

• The ability to work independently or within a group.

• Very good change management skills (explained in more detail below).

• The ability to conceptualise and recommend a potential solution.

Beyond this, let's look at some additional skills in more detail.

The Ability to Translate Users' Needs

A Business Analyst is a listener; someone who can sit and talk to the end-users, and converse with them in a way that will help to identify and define business problems in a clear and unambiguous way. They are **translators**; collating information and finally taking their findings and presenting this data in a more technical format to steering committees and higher beings, ultimately to enable IT management and the IT Director to reach a well-informed judgment as to whether or not to proceed with the modification of their IT system. They are truly the **interface** between the business and the IT department, so although they need to be technologically aware, BAs are brought on for their strategic understanding of the way businesses operate and how technology can help the business move faster towards its key objectives.

Thinking back to my own time in IT recruitment, some of the easiest BA placements I ever made were simply ex-stockbrokers who had had enough of being at the pointy end of the business on the trade floor. Those who had a *penchant* for technology could, with a little effort, combine this with their business background to become high-flying BAs in the investment-banking arena. This said, BAs of course may also originate from a technical background having worked in some form of computing discipline, or indeed have beaten a path straight from an IT-based degree.

The Ability to Gather User Requirements

The first step in any project is to get a clear picture of how the current IT system is working and which problems might currently exist. BAs use a number of techniques to obtain this information and to assess the effectiveness if existing business processes. A key point, which needs to be made here is that, regardless of the pressures placed upon them at this time, it is important for a BA to go into this type of investigation without any preconceived ideas.

Ways in Which BAs Collect Information

There are four key ways of collecting information and these are listed below:

*   **Asking questions directly to the users.** This could be done through interviews, surveys, email questionnaires, or by setting up a

discussion/ feedback database.

- **Observational studies.** This could involve shadowing a user through their working day, or participating directly within the user environment.

- **Dry prototyping.** This means actually trying out the high level ideas at a basic level with a simple model.

- **Formal sessions.** This includes formal workshops, focus groups and facilitated workshops.

User Interviews and Workshops

As mentioned above, BAs and SAs should be very comfortable in carrying out **User Interviews**. Traditionally, this is has been the realm of the systems analyst and is the stage where detailed technical fact-finding takes place. These findings revolve around

- Current processes.

- Data and documents currently used.

- Problems with the current way of working.

- The user's perception of what they require from the new system.

User interviews are generally face-to-face sessions and are an excellent way of obtaining detailed feedback about all of the above points. User workshops are also carried out to ascertain from the user their requirements of a new system. Very often these workshops will involve users from all of the different departments affected by the system. This type of workshop is useful in that it looks at how the data output from one department affects another department. This is known as a **Joint Requirements Planning (JRP)** workshop.

Note: BAs and SAs in these early stages of User Requirements gathering are often viewed with suspicion by departments and users. Companies generally have to go to great pains to make it abundantly clear to all involved as to the purpose of the observation. In many cases workers and trade unions tend to become suspicious of the direct observation and so extra emphasis also has to be made on communicating the fact that it is the *job* being observed and not the person performing the task.

Inside a Feasibility Study

Overview

As mentioned previously, a feasibility study is conducted to justify potential change and check the viability of the proposed remodelling of the business. It is often an essential stage prior to any major business transformation project and, depending on its urgency and complexity, can be thought of as a mini stand-alone project in itself.

Defining the Project Scope

Before a corporation can indulge in even an inkling of thought regarding new and creative IT endeavours (even at the early stages) the decision makers need complete clarity as to the current state of affairs. This process of producing a clear statement regarding the current business environment, and the context of the new project in relation to it, is known as the **Project Scope,** and this is one of the first tasks of a BA. Within the project scope there is just enough information to understand the business needs which have sparked the request for the new system, and the scope of work which must be performed to deliver a product which might satisfy those inadequacies. There isn't a great amount of solutions-oriented advice within this document, but far more emphasis on project planning, estimating and scheduling; enough to give clear indications regarding time and cost projections for the project. The project scope also defines business objectives, possible constraints, expected deliverables (a description of expected products at a high level) and a statement of the anticipated work effort which might be needed. This latter group of considerations is often defined under the sub-heading of the **Business Case**.

Note: It seems fairly evident that the construction of a project scope requires many of the skills which we would normally associate with a seasoned project manager. For this reason, in large and potentially mission-critical projects, the BA may be fortunate enough to have at his/her disposal an experienced Project Manager, a senior developer (in the case of software projects), or even a resident Technical Architect to help with project scoping activities. The resulting team, which sees scheduling and technical experts coalescing and coming to the aid of a BA in this manner, is often referred to as a **Project Proposal Team**. Unsurprisingly, BAs themselves start to develop many strong PM capabilities through this experience and for this reason, we often see BAs pursue the role of Project Manager later on in their career.

Allocating Work Packages with WBS

This feasibility stage of the project starts to define the workload that may be involved in the project, and even begins the process of breaking down the workload into smaller manageable units of work. This process of **decomposition** of workload into smaller units is another abstraction from the world of project management; the technique is often referred to as a **Work Breakdown Structure (WBS)**. The basic idea of a WBS is simply to break a large body of work into smaller and smaller, less daunting, tasks.

BAs Revamping the Recruitment Industry in the 80s

For example (and bringing the theme home for a while), many HR departments and recruitment consultancies in the early 1980s brought in a BA to answer the following question

"Is it worth us bringing in some form of IT system to help us become more competitive in our recruitment process (i.e. in matching clients to candidates)?"

At this stage, from some of the younger readers... (the official definition of 'young' is those who own an iPod Nano, have never bought an album on cassette, and have never heard of Spandau Ballet) ... I'd expect to hear a characteristic

"Duu-uuh – Obviously!"

Yes, it might seem surprising that a question with such an obvious answer even needed to be asked, let alone have extensive sessions dedicated to developing a WBS. But BAs around the world were starting to work on this 'conundrum' in the late 1980s. They came back with a WBS production (occasionally known as a **Scope Decomposition**) which might have looked something like the one below.

The **Top-level WBS** hierarchy for this project might look like this:

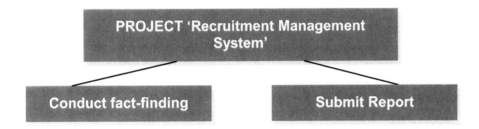

On of these two stages might then be broken down into logical sub-divisions for the **Second-level WBS** as follows:

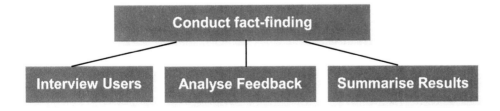

And on to the Third-level WBS as follows:

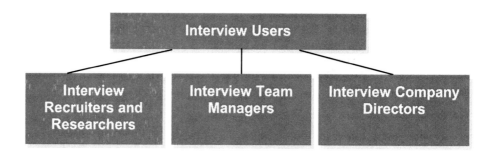

And so on.

You can't really expect to be taken seriously as a BA or SA if you haven't mastered WBS techniques.

The Deliverables of a Feasibility Study

The Resulting Documentation

The results, arising from all of the above activities during the Feasibility Stage, are collated and presented in a formal document. This is referred to as either the **User Requirements Document (URD)**, **Business Requirements Document (BRD)** or even the **Feasibility Report**. Whatever name we choose to give it, the resulting documentation from the Feasibility stage will generally include:

*   An Executive Summary containing strategic plans and goals.

*   The sources of information (users, people who attended workshops etc.) including organisational structures, and business units.

*   A clear description of the current system, with a business problem and opportunity statement.

*   An indication of the weaknesses of the current system (failure rates, downtime, bottlenecks etc.).

*   Recommendations for improvement.

*   Data flows and business processes for each business unit.

*   Organisational charts.

*   Financial metrics.

*   Statistical information relating to all findings.

*   Charts and diagrams where appropriate.

*   Potential Technology Impact Analysis.

Concepts and Technologies Associated with this Role

- **Business Process Reengineering (BPR)** is the art of looking at an organisation's workflow or dataflow; and remodelling it to make it more efficient and effective. Today the term 'BPR' can be applied to any technique or methodology which achieves the above.

- **Change Management** is precisely what it sounds like; the management of change. Though simplistic in its title, this is a complex and politically-sensitive discipline which will often take years to master. We expect BAs to oversee or initiate change at a technological level. But CM is much less to do with planning which computers go where, or who will eventually get to use the new system; and much more to do with building consensus amongst die-hard technophobes and nurturing buy-in from a sceptical user-base who have always done it *the old way*. Change management, in effect, is the slow coaxing of individuals and departments into a way of working that is foreign to them; a gentle soothing influence in the midst of a tumultuous sea of change.

- **Prototyping.** Sometimes the easiest way to see if users will take to a new IT system is to create a scaled-down working model and get them to try it out with dummy data. This is especially useful when testing users' reaction to a new Graphical User Interface (GUI). It can become evident very quickly as users start to play around with the new interface that certain key features are missing from the menu system on the screen. This is also a very good way to prompt users to identify other requirements which they may need from the new system. Though many types of prototyping techniques exist (see page 111 on Iterative Prototyping), the one described above is sometimes known as '**throw-away' prototyping** because the model is only there to aid in the design process and will itself not be carried forward as part of the final solution.

- **Key Stakeholders.** This is a term given to all those parties who may be directly or indirectly impacted by the changes to the business, as brought about by the new or modified system. These may include the;

- Executive sponsors of the new system (i.e. those who initially suggested the change).
- Business process or business unit managers.
- IT Managers supporting the business areas which might be affected.
- Project investment governance group (i.e. the group of senior executives who are directly responsible for funding such modifications within the corporation.

- **Data Flow Diagrams (or Data Modelling).** Whether the client you're recruiting for is an investment bank, an airline or a food manufacturer, all of their internal operations can be represented pictorially or schematically as a group of inter-related processes. Within a recruitment consultancy, for example, one business process may be to match candidates to job specs whilst another linked process will be to pay the contractor their salary at the end of the month once placed. These processes in themselves will have their own sub-processes which make up the whole. **Processes** will always have a **goal** (i.e. assign a pay-rate to a placed candidate). They have specific inputs and outputs and typically will affect many departments within the company. Business analysts and Systems analysts should be very adept at representing business processes in a diagrammatic form using **Data Flow Diagrams**.

- **Computer Aided Software Engineering (CASE)** is a term to define a set of software tools and techniques that help automate and manage the development process. For software developers these tools can simplify tasks, schedule the development, control software versions, and even generate examples of code which might do the job! However, inherently, most CASE tools (such as **ClearCase** from IBM Rational) are also perfect for helping visualise the flow of data, and create data flow diagrams. And so for this reason, they are amongst the most beloved of software tools in the armoury of most BAs and SAs (and for that matter even programmers and architects).

- **Unified Modeling Language (UML)** Although defined as a language, UML is actually an international standard for tools and languages which comply with the original 'UML standard'. UML based tools have a heavy bias towards graphical modelling, and are used to visualise and conceptualise software systems. As a result they are often seen on the CV of analysts as a tool for data modelling, but also on the CV or programmers who use it to conceptualise and automate much of the development process.

- **Entity Relationship Diagram (ERD).** Also known as an **Entity Relationship Model (ERM)** or **Logical Data Structure (LDS)**, this is another data modelling technique as mentioned above. Once again, CASE tools such as ClearCase may be used to generate ERDs, and this term might often be heard when BAs are describing their past experiences.

Interviewing Business and Systems Analysts

The following are good items of conversation to start sorting out the strong from the weak:

- Ask about their overall experience with BPR and change management in their previous roles.

- Who were the members involved in the Joint Requirements Planning workshop (or were they on their own)?

- What experience have they had of data modelling and what was their preferred approach for this?

- Where in their CVs do they make reference to their experience with CASE tools?

- Have they ever had to recommend that a project *does not proceed?*

- Ask them to describe their experience in facilitating user workshops.

- What was their experience of using prototyping approaches during the feasibility stage.

Summary

Prior to reading this chapter, you might have been forgiven for thinking that the analyst role was pretty much a straight forward one-dimensional affair which had its primary focus on mingling with the disenchanted users within a company. But I'm hoping, from the brief glimpse I've given you into the activities associated with the feasibility stage of the project, that there is much more to this role than meets the eye. Analysts are 'mini project managers', excellent team leaders, proficient data modellers, and affective communicators. And of course, in an interview situation we need to assess how the candidate you're speaking to measures up to these high standards.

PART

RECRUITING
SOFTWARE DEVELOPERS

CHAPTER THIRTEEN

Meet the Software Developers

Introduction

Or "I can C clearly now the code has run..."

Even if it's the dreaded 'graveyard' session following a sumptuous conference venue lunch; even if the air conditioning to the training room has packed up for the afternoon, I still find that they sit up and pay the utmost attention as soon as I mention this particular topic. And it's hardly surprising. You can't really get involved in IT recruitment without bumping into the CV of a software programmer somewhere along the way.

"You said I should spend more time with our children, so I turned their faces into icons."

And, of course very soon into their careers, recruiter's and IT HR secretly begin to ask themselves the questions that really matter. Questions such as

"What do these people actually do when they're sitting at their computer screens all day?"

Or

"What does a programming language look like?"

And

"What's so damn special about Java anyway, that these guys get SO excited?"

That, my little *Padawan techno-recruiter*, is where we're going with the next few chapters.

But before we plunge into the whole area of how to recruit software developers, it's worth reminding ourselves of a few of the fundamental concepts relating to software and how it's put together first. This chapter therefore is included as a simple primer, extracting all of the important software-related information from Chapter 3 which we will need to be at ease with before we can even think about mixing it with members of the software development community.

The Three Layer Model of IT: A Recap

Reviewing our simple model of IT in chapter three, we said that the systems which we'll come across in IT can be best represented as a three-layer model with hardware sitting right at the bottom. On top of this is installed an operating system which brings all of the components of the hardware to life and which also readies the computer for the all essential application software (which is the stuff that users actually think of as the worthwhile part of the system such as word processors, email etc.)

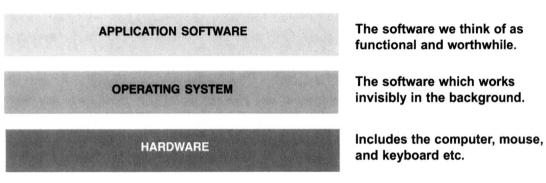

APPLICATION SOFTWARE — The software we think of as functional and worthwhile.

OPERATING SYSTEM — The software which works invisibly in the background.

HARDWARE — Includes the computer, mouse, and keyboard etc.

Figure 13.1
The Three Layer
Model of IT.

Introducing the Programmer Role

"Thirty seconds…"

I peer into the audience and whisper.

"Thirty seconds is all it should take for you to scan a programmer's CV… and understand what it is all about. What they do, which part of the application this candidate has developed and whether they are truly the super-creators of elegant code that they claim to be."

The sniggers give away a healthy scepticism of what has just been claimed. But half an hour or so later, after we've finished the session, there is a silence and they nod in agreement.

Similarly, in the remainder of this chapter we should clear away any early misconceptions you might have when it comes to software development, whilst at the same time laying some strong foundations for the *heavier* stuff to follow.

What's in a Name?

Firstly, you'll note that during much of this section of the book I'll be using terms 'software developer', 'programmer', 'analyst programmer' and 'software engineer' interchangeably with an almost casual disregard for the subtle distinctions between them. Generally speaking the differences are so minute that it's not worth going into it in any great detail. Historically 'programmer' or 'software engineer' is a term associated with the archetypal 'core techie' who wants nothing to do with wearing suits and attending meetings with users or TAs. Similarly the term 'Analyst Programmer' has been assigned to programmers who actually do have a flair for seeing beyond their own little unit of code and are quite happy to liase with others throughout the project lifecycle. However these definitions have certainly become blurred over the years. So for the time being let's allow ourselves to use terms like 'programmer' and 'developer' in an interchangeable way.

For Your Programming Candidates – It's All About Developing the Application Software

Important: When you place software developers into a role with one of your clients, they'll primarily be called upon to develop **application software**. The banks, pharmaceutical and manufacturing companies who hire form you, rarely (if ever) bring in programmers to do anything radical to their in-house operating systems. There are two reasons for this. Firstly, the programming geniuses down at Microsoft and the various Unix vendors have already shipped out a complete operating system along with the hardware which your clients purchased. Secondly, if your clients are a using closed operating system such as Microsoft Windows, they won't be able to access the real workings of the code in order to make any substantial difference to the way it works. Generally, your programmers will be hired by companies to develop the useful, constructive software which we fire-up everyday to enable us to be more effective in business or to make our lives easier. It's this group of software that allows us to write letters, manage our finances, send emails, and match jobs to the right candidate profile on our database. For us to understand software developers we must first understand the structure of application software itself.

So let's get that out of the way now.

How Application Software is Put Together

When you set off to recruit software programmers there are two key things to remember at the outset. Once you grasp these two principles, everything else falls nicely into place.

Firstly: All software applications are constructed in a **three layer approach** as shown below.

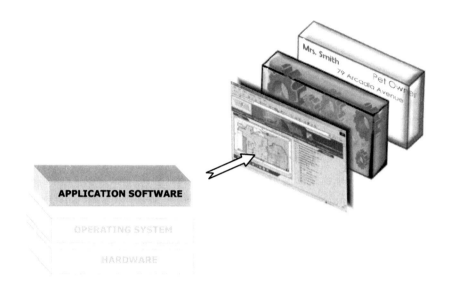

Figure 13.2

Secondly: Software developers tend to specialise in developing *one particular area* of the application (i.e. one of these three layers) rather than the whole application; and this will ultimately categorise them as being either a specialist **front-end** or **back-end** programmer.

So it should be dawning on you that in order to appreciate what software developers really do, we need firstly to be at ease with this layered model of software. Let's do that now.

> *"Programming today is a race between software engineers striving to build bigger and better idiot-proof programs, and the Universe trying to produce bigger and better idiots. So far, the Universe is winning."*
>
>   *Rich Cook – Programming Guru*

A Closer Look at the Three Layer Application Software Model

Most application software consists of

Layer 1 – The User Interface

- This is the part of the software which you and I see on screen when we fire up an application.

- Programmers who develop this are of an application deal solely with how the user is going to interact with the software. For example;

- How will the application appear to the user on the screen?

- How will the user input data (through drop-down menus, radio buttons etc.)?

- How will results be displayed back to the user (through display fields etc.)?

- This layer is known as the **User Interface**, but since most of today's applications make use of a mouse-driven *'point and click'* type interface, we usually call this the **Graphical User Interface** (or **GUI**).

Layer 2 – The Business Logic

- This is the part of the application which deals with what happens **once you've clicked** your mouse button. When we activate an icon or menu item on the screen, we are actually asking the application to carry out a certain task for us. This must draw upon the deeper, layer within the program which then goes to work. This is the layer of the program where all the *real work* is done. In this area of the program all of the tricky calculations take place and mathematical procedures (**algorithms**) are constructed; and is the part of the application often referred to as the **business logic** layer.

Layer 3 – The Data Store

- This is the storage part of any application, and the area where data is momentarily kept on a short-term basis (i.e. for the duration of a calculation) or on a long-term storage basis (i.e. as in the case of a database.)

There we are. That's the basics of programming out of the way; an overview of how software is actually constructed at a conceptual level. After the summary overleaf, we pick up the pace again because, *now* we are ready to start probing deeper into the mind of a programmer. So read on without delay.

Figure 13.3
The Three Layers of an Application Software.

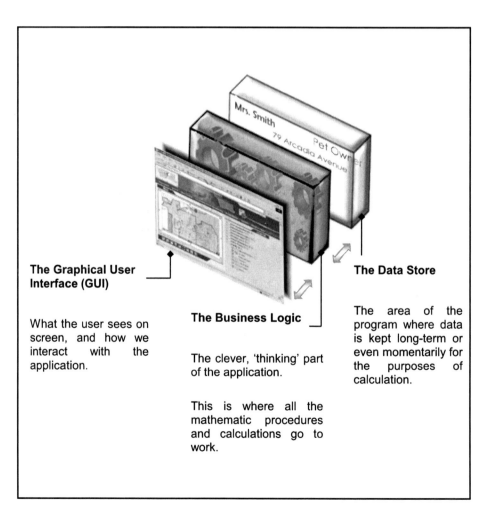

The Graphical User Interface (GUI)

What the user sees on screen, and how we interact with the application.

The Business Logic

The clever, 'thinking' part of the application.

This is where all the mathematic procedures and calculations go to work.

The Data Store

The area of the program where data is kept long-term or even momentarily for the purposes of calculation.

Defining Front and Back-end Programmers

Your clients, whichever sector they may represent, will always be looking to develop newer and newer application software to enhance their existing IT system, augment their business processes, or to enable their employees to work more efficiently. If you recall, what we also said earlier was that all application software is constructed in a three-layer model, as shown below.

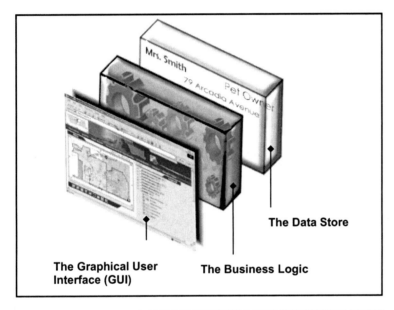

The Data Store

The Graphical User Interface (GUI)   **The Business Logic**

Figure 13.4

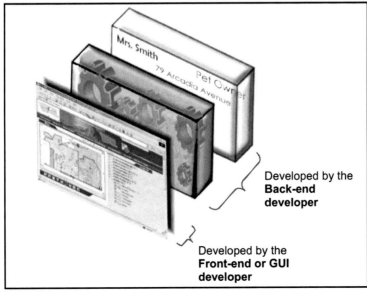

Developed by the
Back-end developer

Developed by the
Front-end or GUI developer

Figure 13.5

We also said that programmers tend to specialise in developing one of these areas of the application; and depending on which area of the application they focus on, we can class programmers as being either **front-end** or **back-end developers**. Here is how we classify them.

Programmers who class themselves as **back-end developers are more focused on the clever thinking part** of the software. They are often requested first by your clients because they put together the fundamental structure, or the thinking, working heart of the application. This can also include the design of the data store area, controlling how the application will store and manipulate data during its day-to-day operations. Of course once the core of the application is constructed, your clients will come back to you in search of front-end programmers to design the user interface. So, **front-end developers are specialist at creating an intuitive and attractive means of interacting with the clever part of the program**, or the Graphical User Interface (GUI).

But the next question is, of course, *how will you know?* How can we tell from looking at a CV whether a programmer is a front-end or a back-end programmer?

Well. **It's all to do with the languages which the programmers choose to become expert in** as they progress throughout their career.

And that is where we are going now as we head into the next few chapters. From here we start delving into the role of front-end and back-end developers in much more detail and begin to explain exactly what each of these do, and which languages they work with in order to achieve their aims.

Summary

So that's the simple stuff out of the way. Now that we have a firm footing we're in a position to move onwards and upwards towards a far greater understanding of the role of the software developer. In the next few chapters we begin our intrepid journey into the mind of the 21st century programmer — both front-end and back-end specialists. We'll start off gradually, but very soon find ourselves up against the more surreal, advanced stuff such as Java and C# programming, Objected-Oriented development, and real-time embedded development.

No need to feel anxious. Remember, The Guide is all patient, The Guide is on your side. Let's read on and find out what a front-end programmer really does.

CHAPTER FOURTEEN

Recruiting Front-End Developers with Visual Basic.NET and Other GUI Tools

Introduction

So how can we spot whether or not a programmer is a front-end (GUI) developer from their CV? Well that's surprisingly easy, and it has everything to do with the languages they tend to use. There are languages which are used specifically to create the GUI part of an application.

The secret, for recruiters, is to be aware of these languages, and then it becomes a relatively easy task to classify a CV as being predominantly front-end or not.

"There aren't any icons to click. It's a chalk board."

These languages are usually easy to spot because they often have 'visual' in their title i.e. **Visual Basic.NET** or **Visual C++** (though this is certainly not a hard and fast rule).

Note: At this point I should also mention that the term 'front-end developer' is also increasingly being applied to web development. We'll tackle web development later on in this chapter, and you'll see that there are a group of languages and applications (i.e. HTML, Dreamweaver, Flash etc.) which are used purely for the purposes of designing attractive web sites. There is also Quick Glance Summary sheet coming up which highlights the key front-end languages and tools you should be aware off.

What Do Front-end Developers Actually Do?

We've already established that front-end developers are those people who are able to make the most complicated piece of software somehow appear easy to use and almost inviting to the novice user. No easy task. They adorn an otherwise complex and complicated program with the attractive menu systems and icons which we are happy to use everyday.

When one imagines a front-end programmer creating the visual part of an application, it is tempting to assume that they are 'programming' in exactly the same way as developers programming in say C++ or Java. However this isn't strictly correct, as we shall soon find out.

We also refer to GUI development *languages* but in reality most of these front-end products (such as Visual Basic.NET or Visual C++) are such **high level languages** (i.e. less technical, easier and more intuitive to use) that they could better be described as visual development *toolboxes* rather than true languages. Let's find out a bit more about that before we move on.

GUI Design Tools

Nowadays the stunning front ends we associate with most software are developed using **GUI toolboxes** or **Widget Toolboxes**, with the term widgets applying to those items we commonly seen on the screen (i.e. buttons, menus, scroll bar etc.) After all, when you actually get your first glimpse of the working screen of Microsoft Visual C++ (shown below) it becomes evident that GUI development, at it's most simplistic level, is very much about dragging and dropping the items you need from the toolbox and directly onto a blank canvas.

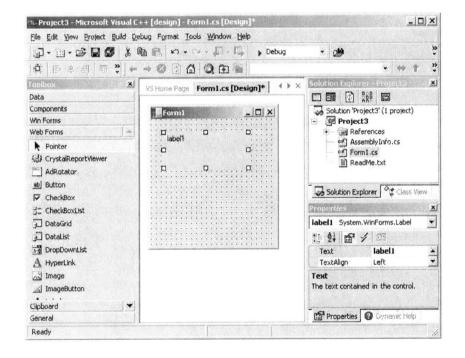

Figure 14.1
Starting point of GUI design in MS Visual C++.
Courtesy: Microsoft Corporation.

The front-end programmer using Visual Basic.NET has at their disposal a range of in-built capabilities and ready-made components (button, check box, drop-down list, or scroll bar). Their focus is never on *creating* the actual buttons or backgrounds from scratch, but on arranging the various components in a logical format for the user.

So dragging two buttons onto the working area and then running the form would result in something that might look like this.

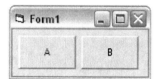

Each component is then allotted characteristics and properties, and of course is assigned specific events to occur when the user hovers over them or activates them in some way (as shown below).

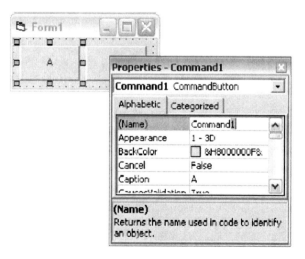

And, once all of the buttons, fields, tabs and checkboxes are organised; with corresponding events and attributes assigned to them – it just remains to 'compile' or '**run**' the program and test that everything works correctly.

GUI toolboxes come in varying forms and from a number of different vendors. Some are proprietary products and others open-source (which are also generally free to use). Below are some of the GUI design elements from an open-source toolbox below. You can see that there are great looking radio buttons, drop-down menus and even icons which a GUI developer can freely use.

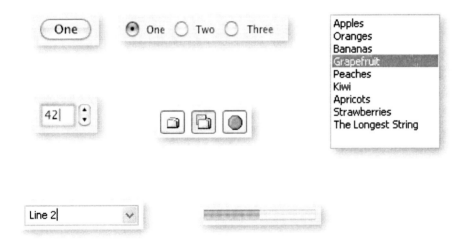

Figure 14.2
Widgets for GUI design.

Courtesy: Open Source.

Is GUI Development Really that Simple?

Of course from what I've described so far, front-end development is now beginning to sound a bit too much like child's play. It appears that all you do is go out and buy a visual development tool like VB.NET. Thereafter, you drag and drop the needed widgets across to your awaiting interface and, *Voila!* You're ready to go.

Surely there must be a bit more to this GUI development lark than meets the eye, otherwise we'd all be at it!

Absolutely.

Key Aspects of the Front-End Development Role

There are of course a number of reasons why front-end developers around the world are paid the fairly healthy daily rates they are by your clients. Creating a GUI isn't just a matter of laying out widgets and icons onto a blank grey canvas in a way that is visually pleasing.

The first of these reasons is that it can be an incredibly long and arduous task to come up with the most effective yet aesthetically compelling 'facia' for the new application software. Front-end developers will sit with members of the back-end programming teams who wrote the business logic part of the program, and in most cases even sit with the business/systems analysts who originally consulted the users about this new system. They may then get involved with the design of and intuitive and user-friendly screen that will feel comfortable to the business users who will be at the steering wheel of this product every day. In most cases front-end developers will also need to assign (sometimes complex) coding to each of the GUI 'widgets' to ensure that each item is invoking the right parts of the business logic before finally presenting the GUI, in a pleasing layout, to the user. As well as all of the above, front-end developers will also

*   Work closely with the Technical Architect to ensure that appropriate front-end technologies are being utilised.

*   Be able to quickly develop prototypes of the GUI for immediate evaluation and feedback from user groups.

*   Oversee user workshops during iterative prototyping feedback sessions (see page 111 for more detail).

*   Ensure that corporate branding is being promoted in the new interface.

*   Ensure that standards and guidelines are being adhered to, and quality benchmarks for the GUI development are set.

Below are a couple of examples of complex GUI interfaces for two completely different industries (a trading system and a design application) that are created using the techniques I mentioned.

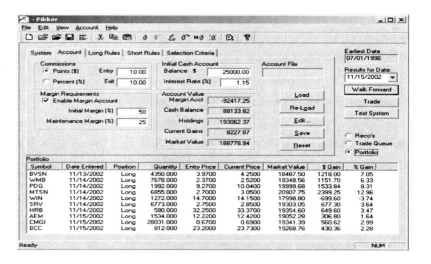

Figure 14.3
Different types of
GUI Interface for
different applications.
*Courtesy: Pikker Software
and 3D Canvas.*

The natural question now is

Which languages do programmers actually use to design these front-end of applications?

With the answer in mind, here is a quick glance summary of some of the front-end development languages and tools of today. You'll notice from the table that Microsoft has a suite of tools which have visual development capabilities. Also note that the GUI development component usually associated with the all important Java (discussed in Chapter 16) is **Swing**.

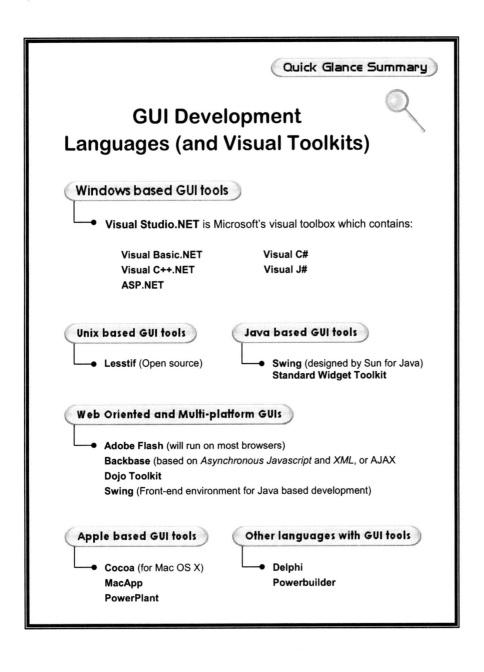

Quick Glance Summary

GUI Development Languages (and Visual Toolkits)

Windows based GUI tools

- **Visual Studio.NET** is Microsoft's visual toolbox which contains:

  Visual Basic.NET   **Visual C#**
  Visual C++.NET   **Visual J#**
  ASP.NET

Unix based GUI tools

- **Lesstif** (Open source)

Java based GUI tools

- **Swing** (designed by Sun for Java)
  Standard Widget Toolkit

Web Oriented and Multi-platform GUIs

- **Adobe Flash** (will run on most browsers)
  Backbase (based on *Asynchronous Javascript* and *XML*, or AJAX
  Dojo Toolkit
  Swing (Front-end environment for Java based development)

Apple based GUI tools

- **Cocoa** (for Mac OS X)
  MacApp
  PowerPlant

Other languages with GUI tools

- **Delphi**
  Powerbuilder

Interviewing Programmers for Front-end Roles

When interviewing programmers for GUI roles it's well worth addressing the following issues:

- Which visual language or toolbox are they most proficient in?

- Have they created their own visual components, outside of the standard library provided in packages such as VB.NET?

- To what extent have they got involved in programming the back-end (highly experienced visual programmer will invariably have acquired fundamental back-end development skills – which always helps when selling in to a client).

- Have they liased with the BA, and did they get involved in coordinating user workshops, and creating prototype interfaces in order to identify needs?

- Also ask them to describe any unique elements which stood out in any of their past projects, this will help to sell them into a client.

- Finally, ask how they might feel if the client prefers a different language to the one they use. Their response to this is usually an indication of how seasoned a visual programmer they are. If they strongly lean towards one vendor, it usually means they haven't really explored a wide range of GUI design situations.

Summary

You now have more than enough information to converse at the appropriate level with most of the mainstream front-end developers you'll meet. Some of these will be individuals who have chosen GUI development tools as a means to get into programming and thus gradually become more proficient in the more techier languages afterwards. But many GUI developers, especially if they have been in the industry for a number of years, simply want to stay as they are; outstanding developers of beautiful user interfaces which enable the most techno phobic of us to easily fire up an application and take it for a drive.

CHAPTER FIFTEEN

Recruiting Back-End Developers with C and C++

Introduction

Whenever it comes to training this topic I tend to leap up from my chair, as I regale tales of Herculean intellects pitted against the most arduous challenges of our time. Yes, occasionally I get passionate about IT (ask any one of the delegates from any given course, and they'll vouch for this without you even prompting them). You might even be forgiven for accusing me of bringing a notably un-British sense of added drama in to play when I narrate some of the key episodes within IT. But I make no apologies in relation to what I have to say about this particular area of IT…which is this.

"Occasionally human beings are capable of such breath-taking leaps of intellectual evolution, that on such occurrences the dazzled onlooker is forced to ask – not

"It's going to rain for 40 days and nights, so God told me to put two of every animal on the ark. And then He gave me something called 'Nintendo' to help pass the time."

"Hey! How they hell do they do that?" but rather
"How the hell did they even dare to think in such an astonishingly unique way?""

Make no mistake about it – that's the sort of realm we're in now when we discuss core programming. These are people who construct explicit complex instructions in languages which they created from scratch; languages that don't really exist outside of the mathematical abstract. They converse with lifeless pieces of silicon using just pulses of electricity or light. And over the years they have quietly gone on to evolve these machines and systems to such a degree that the devices themselves could arguably be considered a minor life form. Simply genius.

Developing the Business Logic

I think it is fairly safe to say (and I'm sure that most front-end programmers won't be offended at this) that *here* is where the real programming wizardry takes place within an application. The back-end is the beating heart of the application where masses of data are analysed and manipulated, multifarious calculations are clinically executed, and mathematical logic is applied.

Back-end development is really the art of developing the clever **business-logic** part of the application, and invariably means that back-end developers are also the ones involved in defining how the raw data is stored, invoked and manipulated, even in relatively simple applications.

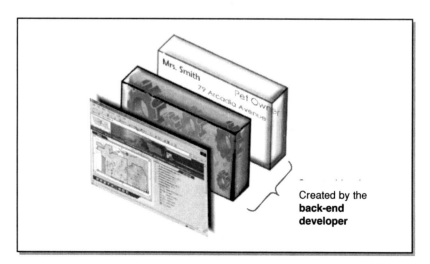

Created by the
**back-end
developer**

Figure 15.1
Back-end
Development.

As a result, these are the very same developers who also get involved with constructing the final layer within an application, the **data management** part of the software. Indeed, if data is going to be the *over-riding* concern within the application, then of course the business logic layer would link directly to a large dedicated database and a **database developer** would be employed in such a case. We look more closely at databases in Chapter 19, so we needn't concern ourselves with that role for now. *All of that in good time.*

High and Low–Level Programming

Programmers in this area of development utilise what are commonly called **third generation languages** (or **3GLs** as discussed in Chapter 15) which are ideal for crafting that complex transactional and process-oriented part of the applications which we all use. 3GL are often referred to as **low-level programming languages.** And to clarify, this term 'low-level' has nothing at all to do with how inferior the language is. In fact low-level programming is far more difficult than high-level programming. Confused? Let's explain.

High-level and low-level programming languages are terms given to indicate **how close the language is to the computer chip's own 'thinking' language** or processing language. As mentioned on page 7, the lowest-level language is the 1GL we call **binary** (or occasionally **machine code**). Current day programmers, with whom you will make contact, no longer program the chip directly in the binary language. That would be far too mind-numbing.

Modern day programmers use languages which are of a slightly higher abstraction and 'easier' to work with; which means that they can write instructions in English, rather than worry about those tedious zeros and ones. Generally, the more *higher-level* language you use, the *less* geeky you're considered to be by other programmers! Java and C can be classed as 3GLs. They use English-type notations so they are higher-level than binary; however nowadays they are still classed as **low-level languages** in comparison to the GUI languages we mentioned in the last chapter.

So Visual Basic.NET (a front-end GUI language) is considered a **high-level 4GL** because it is considered to be easier to use and less *techie* than C or Java. In the simplest scenarios, you don't even need to program using complex lines of code at all with VB. As we mentioned in the last chapter, a large aspect of 4GL programming is the use of pre-made components; making it far simpler to use than any of the 3GLs.

5GLs must, of course, therefore be the highest abstraction away from the computer's own thinking language. Languages such as **Lisp** and **Prolog** are often referred to as **Artificial Intelligence (AI)** languages; which means that the day may soon be upon us when programmers begin their day by sitting in front of a computer and saying something like

"Good morning DellServer 39. Can we re-open Project Traffic Monitoring System where we left off last night ... and turn those display fields back into kilometer format; I had an idea this morning which I think might solve our problem."

And don't assume for a second that this type of concept is way off into the future, it may be closer than you think.

Languages used in Back-End Development

Common languages from the 3GL group, used for back-end development, include:

- C
- C++
- Java
- C#
- Cobol
- Fortran

When you see any of these languages sprinkled liberally across a CV, the applicant is trying to tell you that they are at their happiest when sat in front of a computer screen for eight hours a day typing in hundreds of lines of code!

On A Personal Note – *Curse you Fortran!*

These 3GLs mentioned above were also the first **General Purpose Languages**, meaning that they weren't created with just one particular task in mind but could be used to create a wide range of different applications. These were also the first languages to be given proper names. The first one of these was **FORTRAN** which was developed by IBM in 1957, yet was still a potent enough force in 1990 to be the over-riding bane of my life during my engineering degree. Here it formed an intrinsic part of my final year project, a module towards an aircraft flight simulation package.

To this day I still occasionally wake up in a cold sweat, as dreaded *line 4557* decides to re-visit me in my dream state once again. That devil-spawn line of code, where the mistyped 'o' instead of '0' kept making the ailerons of my Airbus turn to blancmange whenever I banked left! Two days it took us. Three lecturers, that smart Korean kid who knew everything, and myself – and it still took two days to find that error.

I curse you line 4557 – may you never reappear to taunt another poor unsuspecting Aero Eng student!

The Background to Back-end Development

Fortran came first, however it was **COBOL** (**C**ommon **B**usiness **O**riented **L**anguage) which would thereafter become the language of choice for an entire generation of back-end programmers in the 60s and 70s.

It has to be said that some modern-day programmers secretly snigger at these old languages and have even put their own cruel slant on some of the acronyms (i.e. **C**ompletely **O**ver and **B**eyond reason **O**r **L**ogic). This shouldn't detract from the fact that COBOL, in effect, ran our planet's infrastructure for many years and is still far from dead. Many government and military-based systems still rely on this old workhorse, and a surprising number of IT-based functions that currently run our lives are still Cobol-based at the heart of their operation.

Of course many of the old languages have been superseded by newer more innovative 3GLs such as C, C++, C# and Java. All of these have their own unique qualities and a direct claim to their place in the Hall of Fame of modern programming languages. We need to pay them particular attention, which we certainly will do in due course (in fact we'll dedicate a chapter to some of the major ones very soon). But the key thing that should be becoming apparent to you now is that back-end development, on the whole, is a lot trickier and more technologically challenging than developing the GUI part of the application.

After a while in recruitment you'll also come to realise that developers who specialize in this back-end layer will seldom want anything to do with the GUI design side of things. Back-end developers want to focus on the working composition of the program, and then simply move on to another project where they can once again show off their elegant code cutting skills. They'll leave the GUI design part to those individuals mentioned in Chapter 14 of The Guide; i.e. those who have more of a *penchant* towards creativity and an eye for aesthetic. In fact, as I recall from speaking to a number of programmers, there even exists a latent snobbery in programming circles in which programmers using third-generation languages don't always acknowledge 4GL or GUI developers as being *true* programmers. They insist on calling them 'visual *designers*' instead! This all stems from the hard-core techie, pseudo-scientific origins of the low-level 3GL languages. The early 3GLs were convoluted and usually tortuous to work with. Ten different programmers could come up with ten different ways of making one language do the same thing. By the mid-seventies, openly declaring your love for any 3GL language meant that a person had already defined himself or herself as a die-hard 'techie' through and through.

Below is a sample of the sort of thing which might be seen if you glanced over the shoulder of a busy C++ programmer

```
template <class OP1, class OP2>

inline compose_f_g_t<OP1,OP2>

compose_f_g (const OP1& o1, const OP2& o2) {

    return compose_f_g_t<OP1,OP2>(o1,o2);}} /* namespace boost */

#endif /*BOOST_COMPOSE_HPP*/

/* supplementing compose function objects

 * Son Dez 26 22:14:55 MET 1999

 */
```

Pretty, don't you think?

As you can clearly see there is no forgiving, easy-to-use, VB-type interface here to give you that nice welcoming feeling. Just a harsh blank screen, and a keyboard. This level of programming doesn't offer the convenience and simplicity of the drag-and-drop approach. This is *bare-knuckled* programming, using just a keyboard and written commands.

However, as we moved into the eighties, not only did these languages start to evolve, but common **standards** of programming also started to be considered. The **techniques** with which we could use them also started to evolve. Weird and wonderful programming methodologies and approaches started to appear. Concepts like **Object-Orientation**, **Rapid Application Development** and **platform-independence** were starting to be bandied around. Programming was about to enter a new era. In the remaining part of this chapter we're going to look at how the back-end developers use some of the iconic languages of the third generation.

Let's start with the iconic **C.**

Development in C

The History of C

Although you may not find yourself recruiting an overwhelming large number of C programmers today, make no mistake about it. C was a hugely important programming phenomenon when it was launched, and to this day still makes its presence felt. Many programmers refer to C as the 'mother of all modern languages' simply because the fundamental constructs of many modern programming languages such as (C++, Java and C#) are based upon the C way of programming (otherwise known as it's **syntax**). C was originally developed around 1972 by Dennis Ritchie at the AT&T Bell Labs (of the 'transistor fame' mentioned on page 12). It was named 'C' because it was based on an earlier language called 'B', a stripped down version of an even earlier language called **BCPL (Basic Combined Programming Language)**. But don't worry, neither B or BCPL will be turning up on a CV near you in the imminent future.

There are a number of accounts relating to the creation of C, and many of them now almost fade into folklore and legend. However most IT historians agree that the development of C was inextricably linked to the development of another legend of IT; the Unix Operating system. (Unix is discussed in detail in Chapter 5 of The Guide.)

The original Unix was constructed in a form of assembler so that it could only run on one particular machine. However when a new mainframe was ordered (by Bell), there arose a need to develop a new version of Unix which could be ported easily across to this new device. It was then decided that the **kernel** (the core) of the Unix system be written in C to bring about this portability. Since then many other operating systems followed suit, and C soon became the most popular language for writing systems software.

Of course, as time went on, programmers started to use C widely to create application software as well as operating systems. During the late 1970s, C began rapidly to replace Basic as the language of choice for the new microcomputers, and around the 1980s C also started to dominate programming on the newly launched IBM PCs. This would give C the boost into mass recognition, and lay the ground for a new generation of C based languages.

Key Innovations Which Came About With C

In those early days C revolutionized programming because:

*   It made it easier to port Unix across to different computers, and eliminated the need to re-write the whole operating system again from scratch in an assembler language.

*   It made it easier for future generations of programmers to improve and customize software without the need for complicated low-level programming.

*   It encouraged machine-independent programming (which meant that languages were no longer created with just one particular computer or application in mind).

*   It was very fast in comparison to other similar languages of the day.

The C syntax had set the benchmark for software development across the world, and many of the programmers you recruit today will be programming, if not in C, in a language that is directly derived from it. However, in the early 1980s a new generation of gifted programmers had already decided to build upon it's basic principles and pursue far more elegant and sophisticated ways of writing code.

Enter **Bjarne Stroustrup** and **C++**.

The Genius of C++

Still in Bell Laboratories, around 1980, a gifted Swedish programmer called **Bjarne Stroustrup** started to work on how C could be evolved to the next level. Stroustrup wanted to pursue the idea of re-using lumps or modules of pre-written code within a program.

Surely, he reasoned, it would be a more efficient way or programming if developers could take an existing piece of code (an 'object' let's say) and re-use it or indeed the entire family from which it came from (its 'class'). These objects and classes wouldn't need to necessarily be created specifically for a particular project. A completely unconnected programmer might already have written them for another software project, from another company, or indeed another country. But as long as these 'objects of code' satisfied key criterion i.e. that they didn't *freak out* when ripped out from one program and inserted into another, and that they didn't fall apart when you needed to tweak them; then that could work as a new way of programming. The concept of **Object-oriented** C or '**C with Classes**' was born. The new language was coined **C++**; and this would change programming forever.

> There are various explanations as to how the '++' part of the name came about. But in his book 'The C++ Programming Language' Stroustrup referred to 'Doubleplus' which was a term from the fictional language 'Newspeak' from George Orwell's novel 'Nineteen Eighty-four'. In the novel Doubleplus was a term that meant 'extremely technical'; and so C++ can be thought of as the extremely technical mutation of C.

TRIVIA

Recruiting Object-Oriented Programmers

Very often your clients will be happy to pay a hefty premium for developers who can create software using the **object-oriented (OO)** approach. And it is important that you appreciate why. The problem is, if you ask a seasoned programmer to explain the concept of object-oriented development; you'll find yourself slipping into a comatose state as they fire out phrases like:

"Well you see it's all to do with the polymorphistic and multi-inheritance capability of objects and the modular nature of the instances and states which their classes and sub-classes are likely to exhibit".

Don't worry. I'll try and take it more gently.

Here is the key thing to remember about OO programming:

*Object-oriented development is the art of **re-using** pieces (or **objects**) of code which have been already been written by another programmer.*

Why re-invent the wheel! If someone has already created a beautiful, elegant piece of code which does exactly what you need it to do – then why not bring that component into your program.

These objects can be obtained from various sources. They can be purchased from specialist companies selling them on the Internet, or even from fellow programmers. Some objects also come with the language package itself (Microsoft **Visual C++** comes with **MFC** or Microsoft Foundation Classes. 'Class' is another term for a library of objects, and this one is provided for free so that VC++ OO programmers can get a head start with pre-made components). Other objects may be so specialist in their nature that they may need to be created from scratch by the programmer, because they simply don't exist already.

Interviewing C, and C++ Developers with Object-Orientation

In this first decade of the 21st century, the languages which many of your clients will be looking to recruit for are Java and C#, but don't be fooled into thinking that the C and C++ era is at an end. C++ is still going strong because of its awesome track record.

When recruiting back-end developers, remember:

- Ask programmers to summarise the kind of business logic development projects they have been involved in.

- Ask your programmers if they have had experience of object-oriented development. Those with over five years exposure to OO programming will command serious respect from your clients. The truly object-oriented languages in the mainstream are **C++, Java, C#** and **VB.NET**.

- Just because a programmer claims to be proficient in an OO language, it doesn't necessarily mean that they are expert in using that language in an object-oriented way. *A C++ programmer isn't automatically an OO programmer!*

- Generally new entrants to the programming industry have very little exposure to using languages in a live visceral OO environment. You need to ask candidates in order to make sure!

- The methodologies on your programmer's CV will always be a strong indicator as to whether or not your candidate can work in an OO way or not. We're looking for those with OO in their title such as **OOAD** (OO Analysis and Design), but also the other big three OO methodologies which are **Booch, Coad-Yourdon** and **Rumbaugh**.

- Occasionally you'll come across candidates who develop in **Visual C++** and **Visual C#**. These are languages with which a developer can create both the front **and** back-end of an application. Make sure that you're not faced with a candidate who is trying to come across as a core techie back-end developer, but in actual fact has only dabbled with the front-end GUI aspects of these languages.

The best way is to simply ask

"Did you primarily use this as a GUI tool, or were you developing back-end elements of the application software using this language?"

Well reader, that was truly a *Jedi-level* programming concept which we've just discussed, and if it has sunk in – give yourself a pat on the back.

Finally, there's a diagram overleaf to clarify OO further.

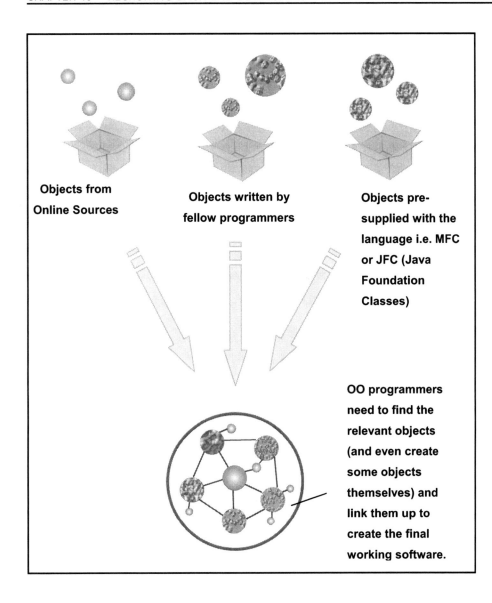

Objects from Online Sources

Objects written by fellow programmers

Objects pre-supplied with the language i.e. MFC or JFC (Java Foundation Classes)

OO programmers need to find the relevant objects (and even create some objects themselves) and link them up to create the final working software.

Figure 15.2
The principle behind object-oriented development.

Summary

So that was a good look into the world of back-end developers and OO. I hope it's made a few things clearer for you. You'll also have begun to realise that there are a number of inherent benefits of going down the OO path, and why many of your clients will be asking for programmers who can run with this approach. This is an exciting area of IT recruitment and you should look forward to speaking with some very talented people indeed.

But, we're not quite finished with OO just yet.

We can't really leave this area without looking in more detail at the most revolutionary OO language of the last decade …. *Java*.

This language us so hot – it needs its own chapter. R*ead on.*

CHAPTER SIXTEEN

Recruiting Java Developers

Introduction

Currently medical science is looking back and re-evaluating the behavioural patterns of exceptionally great minds such as Einstein, Da Vinci and Newton. In speculating about what actually made these people so extraordinary, the experts have arrived at a bizarre new conclusion. Apparently, it wasn't that these guys had superior 'thinking hardware' or even a more abundant supply of it than the average human being. In fact the key attribute which was common to all, was that they possessed uniquely 'defective' and 'malfunctioning' minds. Minds which somehow lacked the filters that most 'normal' people learn to erect as they grow up.

STRAIGHT TO

➤ Before Java
  Page 242

➤ How Java works
  Page 246

➤ Interviewing this role
  Page 250

➤ What we should see on their CVs
  Page 250

➤ Summary sheet
  Page 254

> "The significant problems we have today cannot be solved at the same level of thinking with which we created them."
>
> *Albert Einstein*

This lack of mental screens and filters in essence is what allowed those *beautiful minds* to dare to visualize situations which you and I would never think of dreaming up. Question, such as Einstein's

"What would it feel like to sit on the edge of a beam of light?"

would never have been possible, apparently, without this *defective* ability to think outside of the norm.

Bizarrely, this *imperfection* in their make-up also enabled them to analyse problems with such a clarity that they could also look at solutions from a uniquely different angle. Actually, what the medical experts now agree on is that being able to think outside of the box to this extent is a form of *autism*. In medical terms this extreme phenomenon, of individuals being endowed with such lateral thinking capability, is known as *savants* (from the French, meaning unlearned or 'idiot talent').

So how does that relate to our story here? Well, I'm not implying that Sun Microsystems was overrun with *Rain men* in the summer of 94; but there was certainly an inordinate amount of 'out of the box' thinking that year in one quiet corner of this company. For here, beneath the shade of an ancient oak tree (naturally), an association of ideas never previously pursued by programmers would for the first time be established. And without which we would never have had the creation of … **Java**.

That was a huge build up. But once again I make no apologies. For you see, there is something so very special about Java. When it was introduced to the world in 1995 it was unique. It would be able to do what no other language could previously do. ***It would change the way we view programming forever.***

Let's find out a bit more about this groundbreaking language.

Just Another Vague Acronym?

Java was created in around 1994 in the research labs of Sun Microsystems (a company that was better known for its range of corporate level computer hardware, its SPARC chip architecture and its Solaris operating system) in what came to be known as the **Green Project.** The person heading up the project was a brilliant programmer by the name of **James Gosling** who is now widely credited to be the father of the Java programming language. Internally, within Sun, the new language was also referred to as **Oak** (after the tree that stood just outside of Gosling's office) but this finally had to be renamed due to potential trade marking complications. And so the name *Java* was short-listed.

Some like to think it stands for *Just Another Vague Acronym* but actually it had more to do with the numerous cups of coffee that Gosling and his team drank during this project. There is a far geekier account of the naming story, relating to a string of hexadecimal numbers which resembled '0xCAFEBABE' – but those who really have an unremitting urge to understand this further should email me personally at ithinkiamareallysadgeek@heart.com.

Excuse Me Sir, Which is Our Platform?

Gosling and his team were becoming increasingly frustrated with one particular limitation associated with the programming languages of the day, which was this. Whenever an application was created in a language such as C, Cobol or C++; programmers would have to, from the outset, design and develop the application **with a particular platform in mind**.

At this point it's probably quite important to define the term **platform** clearly for those of you haven't really had a chance to think this through. In an IT sense the term 'platform' refers to the combination of the bottom two layers of our IT model, so the combination of the operating system and hardware.

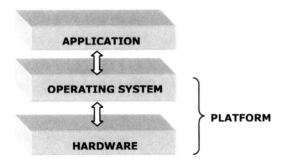

Up until this point, all previous languages (C, Fortran, Pascal, C++ etc.) were **platform-dependant**. This meant that if a company had just embarked on the creation of a new application, using one of the above languages, they would have had to define **at the outset which platform they were going to create** that program for.

The software product would then be created and could only work on that specific platform. Subsequently if you wanted to ensure that your new application could work on other platforms, well that simply meant a new re-development of your application from scratch many different times (with the associated costs and hassles attached to that process).

The Situation Before Java

Let's think this through. With all pre-Java languages, developers would have constructed the core of the application first which conceptually we can think of as this:

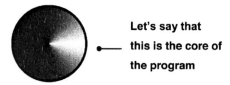

This core thinking part of the program is often called the **bytecode**, and contains all of the clever business logic part of the application.

However the developers would then still need to 'shape' it so that it could then sit on a particular platform. So, let's say initially that this company wanted to target a user-base that ran the MS Windows operating system on PCs.

In which case the application might need to look something like this:

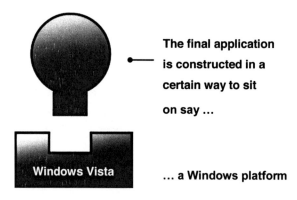

However, if the developers then realized that they also wanted the application to work on other platforms (let's say in order to increase market share), this would mean them redeveloping the product again (often from scratch). A costly exercise, which would result in further versions of the application.

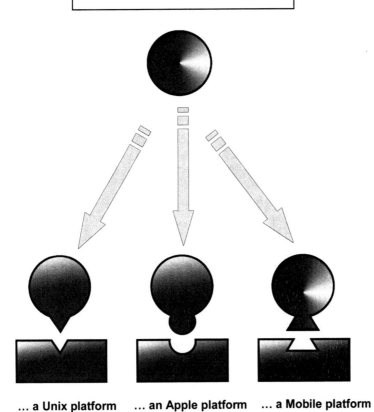

The application would then need to be re-constructed again and again in order to be able to work on ...

... a Unix platform   ... an Apple platform   ... a Mobile platform

Figure 16.1
Re-creating an
application for use
on many platforms.

This has always been a real issue for developers throughout the ages.

And this isn't just a problem for software development houses. All large companies, from investment banks to manufacturing companies, have fallen foul of this syndrome. A large aircraft manufacturer such as Boeing, or a global bank such as Barclays Capital may have, across their entire global IT architecture, over 15 different internal platforms. A branch of the same bank in the Middle East may have, somewhere along the way, purchased different hardware (and operating systems) from another branch in, say Brazil. Each time a new application is created, it may need to be re-developed 15 different times so that the application can work throughout the bank's global infrastructure.

Let's Just Not Do It That Way

Going back to Sun Microsystems, the team on the Green Project found themselves in the same position, but much more so. They were tasked with developing applications for a new generation of small smart devices such as mobile phones and PDAs (Personal Digital Assistants) which Sun thought would very quickly become the dominant personal IT architecture of the future (correctly as it turns out). However it was becoming an increasingly tedious chore to continually re-test, re-design and re-develop applications for each of the different platforms that were available. Each platform, each hardware, each operating system presented its own unique problem for the application development teams.

However, rather then plodding on, the team paused for a moment and thought about this. Asking

*"Wouldn't it be great if we could develop our application **just once**, but it was developed in such a way that it could run on any platform?"*

For the first time they had dared to think the un-thinkable, and the concept of **WORA** was born.

'WORA – Write Once, Run Anywhere!'

They pursued this idea and eventually, against all odds, constructed a programming concept that would allow them to do just that. Program an application in such a way that it could automatically adapt itself to run on all platforms.

Java became the world's first commercially available 'platform independent' programming language.

At this point I'd expect to hear a gasp of *'Wow!'* from the reader. Nothing less will do!

But How Does it Work?

If the idea of even the possibility of such a language was an inspired one, the solution they arrived at was nothing short of genius. How a Java developer goes about building platform-independent languages, that's where we're going now.

How Java Developers Create Platform-Independent Applications

Step 1: Build the core of your program

The idea behind Java development was to build the core part of the application, known as the **Java bytecode**, in the traditional manner. However unlike previous programming languages, the programmer wouldn't need to worry at this stage about platform issues. Java enabled the developer to simply crack on with developing the Java code using the supplied Java Development Kit (explained below).

So again, to keep it simple, the core of the Java bytecode might look (diagrammatically) like this:

The core of the program

But here's the clever bit coming up.

Step 2: Build the all-important 'JVM'

Rather then building the platform information into the core of the program itself, **Java attaches this separately** as a different piece of code; which is divorced from the java bytecode itself.

This element of the Java programming environment was the stroke of genius which the people at Sun came up with; and is the key to Java's platform independence. Known as the **JVM** or the **Java Virtual Machine**, this separate segment of code has only one function, and that is to simply **act as a universal translator for all platforms. The JVM is what makes Java-based applications portable**.

Think of the Java Virtual Machine as a really extreme software version of a universal plug adaptor which frequent travellers buy. A 'totally universal' one might look like this:

In the same way, the Java Virtual Machine, for the purposes of our diagrammatic approach might look a bit like this:

**The Java Virtual Machine (JVM) can be thought
of as a software universal adaptor**

It is an extremely clever, active piece of Java code which is often referred to as a '**machine within a machine**'; and its sole purpose in life is to take and Java bytecode and allow it to sit snugly on a myriad of different operating systems.

Note: The JVM is not the only 'universal software adaptor' available though it is the best known. It is also worth noting that this term '*universal software adaptor*' is my own metaphor to explain this concept to you, and not one that is commonly used in the industry (*just yet!*).

Once the JVM is implemented, the developer can then *simply* bolt it to the Java bytecode and, you have it, your application will then be able to operate on any platform, as illustrated below.

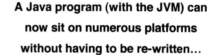

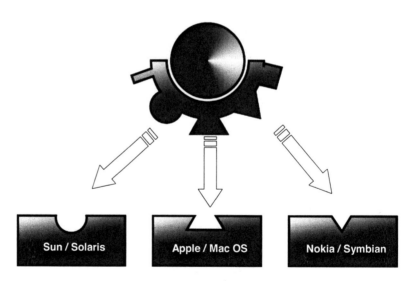

This JVM holds a library of all of the world's mainstream platforms, and as new ones come out, these are constantly being updated. So, in this way Java developers need only write applications once, and they will be able to run on any platform in the world!

So now you know about the wonder of Java. And I'm sure you'll agree when I reiterate a point I made earlier in the last chapter when I said …

"Occasionally human beings are capable of such breathtaking levels of mental agility that one is forced to ask, what was more brilliant …"

Interviewing Java Programmers and Studying Java CVs

That's the hard bit out of the way. However it remains for me to explain the associated technologies and what they mean; so that you can converse more confidently with Java candidates. Listed below are some easy-to-understand explanations of common Java-based terms which may appear on your job requests and on candidates' CVs. Before an interview I suggest you quickly flick back to this section and scan the terms you need to discuss. Since there really isn't a pretty way to package these, I'm just going to lay the key terms out for you, one by one as an easy to read Java-recruiter's glossary. There's a lot of it, but it's all important – so don't be daunted, and enjoy!

Java SE (Previously **J2SE**)

There are a number of variations to the Java language (sometimes referred to as the Java platform). The one that your clients will adopt for their development project will depend heavily on the size and scope of the technical challenge. So for example what we've historically always considered to be the good old fashioned Java language is now referred to as **J2SE** or **Java Platform, Standard Edition** or more recently **Java SE**. For smaller projects and those without a huge amount of complex web-based interaction this is a very competent tool. In fact the components of this basic version are usually good enough for most projects right up to large-scale multi-tier systems, with both real-time and embedded systems.

Java Enterprise Edition (Previously **J2EE**)

For most of your clients, when the development project involves large-scale deployment of a software product over the entire enterprise architecture, most projects turn to **J2EE,** also known as **Java Platform Enterprise Edition** or **Java EE** in its latest incarnation.

Java EE comes into play whenever IT needs to make an impact over a large heterogeneous infrastructure, and where the users might be tapping into massive distributed databases (see JDBC below) via a mixture of both fat and thin clients.

Java EE (not surprisingly) includes all of the components found in Java SE and much more. Within this environment you can create web servers, **application servers** (i.e. those which control and drive the provision of applications to either a web interface or to users over a large network – see Jboss below), and create Java applications that connect directly to databases using Java Database Connectivity (JDBC).

Within Java EE, the programmer can also work with Enterprise Java Beans (EJB), and create applets and servlets – all of which are explained below.

Java Micro Edition (Previously **J2ME**)

If you're a programmer developing for small wireless and mobile devices with minimal memory and limited processing power, such as Personal Digital Assistants (**PDA**), or mobile phones; you would turn to this edition of the Java platform. Java ME is a very lightweight version of the other members of the Java development family, and is therefore suited to a device with minimal storage capability. However it hasn't achieved true *platform-independence nirvana* because there are currently scaling issues in that applications still need to be tweaked to work on different devices when written in Java ME.

JavaBean

This becomes simple to explain if you've understood all we discussed about the object-oriented (see page 237) nature of Java. At its simplest level, a JavaBean is a Java 'object'. JavaBeans are re-usable objects which are dropped into forms and other 'containers' to make up the complete Java program.

Java Applet

Java applets are small self-contained Java mini-programs which often sit within and run inside a larger program. Most often applets are invoked in a Web browser and show up in the form of clocks, calculators, calendars etc. Java applets can be made up of Java beans.

Java Servlet

A Java servlet, *believe it or not*, can be thought of as a Java applet which resides on the server. Its main function is to provide services and data from the server or over the network to a front-end web (or intranet) interface. Servlets are best used for the presentation of real-time or dynamic data to a web page from a back-end server.

JBoss

Jboss is a free software to create application servers using Java. In a large multi-tier network, the application server houses the clever thinking part of the software (business logic).

WebLogic

Although this product wasn't created by Sun; in fact it is owned by BEA Systems (which was started by a group of ex-Sun employees), the WebLogic software is yet another application server software built around the Java EE product.

WebSphere

This is yet another non-Sun product which you will see appearing on the CVs of Java developers. WebSphere was actually created by IBM and is a set of Java-based tools to allow customers to create and manage sophisticated commercial e-commerce web sites. WebSphere also therefore contains the tools to create excellent web servers and application servers. In fact because much of WebSphere's tasks revolves around translating between different platforms, it can be thought of as middleware (see page 166 to better understand the concept of middleware).

Java Development Kit (JDK)

This is the toolkit which Java programmers use to construct Java programs, and is often a subset of the various editions mentioned above (i.e. J2SE, J2EE and J2ME).

JavaScript

JavaScript was created by Netscape and doesn't really have anything specifically to do with the Java platform as such. It is a *scripting* language and therefore, by definition, much easier to program than Java. JavaScript is primarily linked to web site design, and is yet another method of creating active components such as clocks, date functions and other dynamical and interactive content. The only reason I'm mentioning it here is that most of the delegates on my training courses tend to ask about JavaScript during the Java part of an event. However it's worth knowing that very few experienced Java developers will want anything to do with creating JavaScript applications, as this is usually the realm of the web designer.

Swing

Swing is the front-end GUI design toolkit for Java. It contains ready made 'widgets' which front-end developers may use to put together what the user sees at the front end of a Java application.

AJAX

AJAX stands for **A**synchronous **J**avaScript **A**nd **X**ML is yet another tool designed to create dynamic and data-rich web sites. One of the cool things about AJAX is that it uses XML based technology for handling data transfer (eXtensible Mark-up Language is one of the most powerful tools available today for manipulating web-based data). The other benefit of using AJAX over similar tools is that to allows better interactivity because it doesn't rely on the whole web page being reloaded every time the user requests new information.

JSP

Another way of creating dynamic web content (if you didn't want to use just AJAX) is Java Server Pages. This tool however can generate complete pages in HTML with the data you requested.

SOA /SOAP

Simple Object Access Protocol is a very innovative software tool which allows applications sitting on one platform (such as HP-UX) to work seamlessly with programs sitting on another platform (such as Windows) **using the web as a medium to communicate** (more specifically using XML and HTTP). One of the key players in its creation was Microsoft, and it is another software that we could classify as a type of middleware (though some commentators might disagree). Also, by being such an excellent mediator between web-based platforms, SOAP generally has a knack of getting through the firewalls in its way, which might otherwise prevent the data reaching the user.

JDBC

Java Database Connectivity (**JDBC**) allows Java applications to interface with databases. It also works well with **SQL** (Structured Querying Language is the language which all databases use to allow users to 'query' the mass of data they hold), and so allows Java programs to be fully integrated into the key functionality of a database.

Spring

Spring is a Java-like development framework that is designed to work with Java-based technologies. However it stems from the Open Source community (and driven primarily by a chap called Rod Johnson) and so is not controlled by Sun Microsystems. This has now become a popular development environment in large enterprise arenas (such as banks) because it simplifies many of the complicated operations associated with traditional Java tools. Spring uses POJO (Plain Old Java Objects) to achieve its objectives and can replace more convoluted Java technologies such as EJB (Enterprise Java Beans).

Ruby and Ruby on Rails (ROR)

Though not directly linked to Java, Ruby is often seen on CVs alongside. Ruby is an object oriented scripting language from Japan and claims to extract the best of other similar languages such as Perl, Python and Lisp. Ruby is primarily used in high-traffic web applications. **Ruby on Rails (ROR)** is the name given to the development environment or framework based around the Ruby language. ROR automates (or at least simplifies) the creation of many real-time web-based applications such as live-trading and database connectivity.

Perl

Not directly linked to Java, but seen alongside on CVs, Perl is an older general-purpose language created for writing scripts in the Unix environment. Since then its reputation as the 'Swiss Army Chainsaw' of languages has seen it at the heart of a myriad of development environments from web development to graphics programming and of course network administration (reflecting back to its roots).

PHP

Once again not directly linked to Java, but seen alongside, PHP is a programming language which recently has become one of the most popular languages for server-side web operations. In plain English this means it is now far easier for web developers to create pages that can handle on-the-fly web submissions. Immediately displaying forms, inventories and images in real-time as they are submitted is invaluable for content sites such as the BBC or Sky News.

And Finally ... The Microsoft Rebuttal to Java

From what we've just read, it sounds as if the whole platform independence gig was pretty much sewn up by the geniuses down at Sun.

Well, until 2001 this certainly was the case. However, Microsoft was not going to sit quietly on its hands in the midst of what was potentially the biggest evolutionary leap in programming since we stopped coding in binary! And true to form, Microsoft came out fighting, and very quickly released its own response to the Java sensation.

In the next chapter we take a look at an area of software development that will become increasingly important to your clients and candidates alike. If you're not doing so already, you had better get ready to start recruiting candidates for the **.NET development** era.

Let's go there now.

Java: A Summary

Java's Key Attribute

- **Java was developed by Sun and is the first commercially available 'platform-independent' language.**

  This means that programs written in Java can work on any platform. These resulting programs can run on Windows, Unix or even mobile and PDA environments. The edition of Java you use will ultimately depend on the size and nature of the application.

Owned by

- **Sun Microsystems**

Java based GUI tools

- **Swing**
  Standard Widget Toolkit

Java Editions

- **Java EE** (For large-scale applications with web-enabled capability)
  Java SE (For smaller scale and less enterprise capability than Java EE)
  Java ME (For mobile phone and PDA environments)

Java and OO

- Java is also object-oriented, which means that it can be developed around small pieces of code known as 'beans' which are very often extracted from libraries or 'classes'. In this way one can create 'applets' and 'servlets' which behave as mini-applications.

CHAPTER SEVENTEEN

Recruiting C# and .NET Developers

Or The American War of Platform-independence

Introduction

The first year of the 21st century had come and gone. And, to everyone's relief, the long-anticipated attack of the much feared millennium bug didn't actually materialize. The Cobol-based legacy infrastructure around the world simply cantered innocuously and serenely into the millennium without so much as a whimper. The chaos we were expecting, when the 'date' functions in programs around the world changed from '99 to '00, didn't transpire to any great degree and the planet once again regained its trust in IT.

But at the headquarters of Microsoft, the turn of the millennium had brought with it a new and daunting battle. A language, indeed a programming phenomenon, was starting to sweep across the world as a *tour de force* within the coding fraternity. A language so groundbreaking, that it was questioning the very need for other languages. Its name was Java; it didn't originate from the '*big house*'. And that was always a problem.

Microsoft had to deliver a worthy response somehow. And deliver it did. Around the middle of 2002, Bill Gates announced the birth of a concept so big, its significance (in Gates' own words) could be compared to the creation of Windows itself.

Amidst tremendous fanfare, Microsoft's *magnum opus* was launched that year as **C#** (pronounced C sharp) and the **.NET** (pronounced 'dot net')

Framework. In so doing they had thrown their hat into the ring as a key contender in the arena of platform-independent development.

In a .NET briefing on July 24th 2002, Bill Gates described the software challenge behind .NET as

"...one of the toughest software problems ever tackled, easily greater than tough engineering problems like getting to the moon or designing the 747.."

Of course, the problem with being the richest man in the world, and the most recognised figure in IT is that everything you say will be taken literally, and dissected clinically. Inevitably, after the above statement, many in the world of programming scoffed at the above statement as being mere rhetoric in order to enhance a language that was clearly going to be playing second fiddle to Java.

The problem was that, in those early days, not too many people really understood exactly what .NET was meant to be. What was a 'framework' anyway? Was it a platform, or a development tool? As an observer of the IT landscape in those days I must admit I often found the descriptions of .NET slightly confusing. Industry analysts around the world were clambering to write reports about this new 'framework.' However for many of us, as with many new IT concepts, it did bring to mind the ancient fable of the 'Six Blind Men of Indostan' trying to describe an elephant by what they each individually perceived it to be.

For a while .NET felt like a spear, a wall, a rope, a tree, or a snake. Either one of these, or all of these at the same time.

This possibly wasn't helped by a new naming (marketing?) strategy by the software giant, which meant that new versions of many traditional Microsoft products also underwent a re-branding exercise with .NET bolted on as a suffix (products such as VB, and ASP would now be called VB.NET and ASP.NET).

Even today when I ask a recruitment audience what they understand by the term .NET, I am occasionally reminded of the six blind men and the elephant syndrome. One recruiter will say it's a front-end development language (because he's seen it written on CVs as Visual Basic.**NET**), another will say it's a web-site development tool (because she's seen it on CVs as Active Server Pages.**NET**), and another will say it's a scripting language (because she's seen it described in job specs as Jscript.**NET**).

So, it's definitely time to clear away the confusion. In this chapter I'll clarify many of the .NET technologies and concepts associated with the very important area of software development, once and for all. Let's do that now.

Don't worry, as always I'll take it slowly (though experience tells me that we might need to tread even more carefully than usual with this one.)

So what exactly is .NET?

Microsoft **.NET** is a collective or umbrella term for a group of languages, products and technologies which work within the **Microsoft .NET framework**.

So with this rather abstract initial statement we can at least pin down the following points:

* .NET is **not** a language in itself, but a toolbox of development technologies.

- In the context of regular conversation, the term '.NET' and '.NET Framework' mean pretty much the same thing.

Right, next step (stay with me on this!).

The .NET Framework can be thought of as an *operating system enhancement* for Windows so that once you add the .NET framework component to existing Microsoft operating systems they can then benefit from everything which the new .NET technologies have to offer.

The .NET Game Plan

If you speak with some of the more sceptical observers of the IT industry they will emphatically tell you that Microsoft's aim in producing the .NET framework was simply an attempt to regain some of the lost mind share that occurred as a result of the release of Java.

By the year 2000 there was no doubt that Java had quickly become the darling of the IT industry. Object-oriented and based on C and C++ syntax, Java enabled programmers to quickly adapt to it without a steep learning curve. Java also claimed to have solved a lot of the problems and issues of programming with C++ and C (such as improving memory leaks and simplifying over complex programming rules), and of course Java achieved the programming nirvana of platform-neutrality to boot.

The .NET Framework or at least one of its components would need to achieve *at least* most of the above in order to stand a chance of standing out against the trundling and unstoppable Java road show.

Microsoft decided that .NET would be the overall campaign. But **C# was to be the spearhead**; the language to take centre stage as the worthy challenger to Java.

Interviewing .NET Candidates

When a client says

'We're looking for a .NET developer.'

What they are really saying is that they are looking for candidates to develop applications for the .NET environment (*.NET platform*, *.NET framework* – whichever works for you!) using one or more of the .NET family of development tools.

The key .NET technologies which the candidate would be expected to use in the development, will therefore be one from amongst the following:

The .NET Languages (Front-end)

* Visual C#
* Visual Basic.NET (Previously Visual Basic)
* Microsoft Visual C++ (now known as MSVC)

The .NET Languages (Back-end)

* C++/CLI (Common Language Infrastructure)
* C#
* J# (is a transitional language allows Java programmers to use their expertise and experience on the .NET platform)

The .NET Web development and Scripting Tools

* ASP.NET (Previously Active Server Pages)
* Jscript.NET

And you need to be absolutely clear as to which aspects of the .NET environment your client is really looking to develop, and which .NET tools they would like to see being used. In the same vein you need to be completely comfortable in asking your candidate which components of .NET they are most experienced in. Generally if they call themselves a .NET developer they will be referring to C# as their primary tool of choice.

Finally, ask candidates if they have experience of creating platform-independent applications. The reply will always be an interesting one.

Summary

Never has the programming community experienced so much heated debate as witnessed over the last six years following the launch of C#. Those from the Java camp have never relented in mocking the many similarities which C# shares with Java. Those from the Microsoft camp continue their wholehearted support of this latest offing as yet another masterstroke by the undisputed programming genius that is Anders Hejlsberg (the inventor of Turbo Pascal and lead designer in the team that created Delphi). I personally am not going to enter into that debate here (trust me, you'll find plenty of candidates who'll be happy to sway your views one way or the other regarding this topic). However, what I can do is highlight for you the key properties of C# in comparison to that of Java (see Summary sheet). And finally, there is an additional sheet to summarise the key characteristics of the C# programming language.

Now all you need do is find a cracking good C# developer to sit down and have a good natter with; and then sell, sell, sell!

Quick Glance Summary

C# versus Java
- A Comparison

Java	C#
• Is platform-independent.	• Primarily designed for the Windows platform but can also demonstrate platform-independence.
• Uses the Java Virtual Machine (JVM) to achieve platform independence.	• Uses the Common Language Runtime (CLR) to achieve platform independence.
• Is older and so has had a head start in establishing itself with the programming community.	• Relatively new but has therefore had the opportunity to iron out some of the perceived failings of Java.
• Uses Swing for it's GUI or desktop development.	• Uses Visual C# or Visual Basic.NET for it's GUI or desktop development.
• Java Enterprise Edition used with Java Server Pages (JSP) for large scale enterprise deployments with web-enabled capability.	• Microsoft do this through C# with ASP.NET (previously Active Server Pages).
• Can create applets and servlets to be re-used in an OO manner.	• C# uses WinForms and WebForms to achieve the same results.

C#
- An Overview

- It is designed to be platform-independent

- It is similar to Java in its syntax (language structure) so by implication

- It is also derived from C and C++, as well as Java

- It claims to borrow the best aspects of these languages mentioned above, but without inheriting their limitations or drawbacks.

- It is a very good object-oriented language so is designed to be used to create objects or software components that can then be used in a distributed architecture

- Can work equally well on standard computing architecture as well as embedded systems (i.e. mobile phones and PDAs.

CHAPTER EIGHTEEN

Recruiting Software Testers

Or, *Looks good! But does it work?*

Introduction

In a world where new and innovative technologies seem to make a debut every day, and where the IT arena is bombarded by ideas and concepts relentlessly; there is growing pressure to release innovative software to rapidly meet the demands of the day. This holds true for both in-house development projects and for commercial software houses constantly trying to create a new wave of products to wow a very fickle consumer base. However in this hectic environment how does one set standards for quality in relation to such a products? Who ultimately can define whether or not a software product is good enough, and robust enough for general release to the end-user? When asking such questions we have entered the realm of Quality Assurance and software testing.

"I found the problem, Phil...
your spell checker had a nervous breakdown."

What is Testing?

Testing is the process of identifying and correcting errors which might exist in an IT system. Testing is *not* a certification that a system is completely free of errors. It is almost impossible to ensure that the complex software applications of today are 100% bug free. Realistically, testing can only go someway to assuring us that it will perform it's key activities without major errors.

It's also important to appreciate the key difference between software errors and hardware errors. Hardware faults occur, at least in part, because of wear and tear. Hardware components have a greater chance of failing as time goes on. Software faults seldom suffer from the problems of wear and tear but generally arise through initial design flaws.

So, why is there such an emphasis on structured testing? Simply put, there is a simple economic logic to getting it right at the construction stage. Studies over the last ten years have shown that a defect discovered during the early coding stage that costs £1 to rectify will, if un-treated, cost £1,000 to repair later on in mass production.

Why Are There So Many Different Types of Testers?

The thing that becomes immediately apparent when one starts to get involved in recruiting software testers is that there is a plethora of different software testing titles. You come across **white-box testers** and **black-box testers, UAT testers** and **Integration testers, Systems testers** and **Unit testers. Beta testers** and **regression testers**. The list seems endless, but of course it isn't. And, in actual fact it's quite easy to understand these numerous variations once we remind ourselves of the simple logic behind building software in the first place.

Going back to our Waterfall Model approach to building software, true software programming (and therefore testing) can only really start in earnest at the coding or build stage. Prior to this all we have are surveys, concepts, high-level ideas and data models. After the design stage we have a blueprint drawn up by the Technical Architect which in itself is also a detailed design in which programmers must install code in order to breath life into those ideas.

How Testers See the Waterfall Model

Testing of course starts as soon as there is a physical lump of code to test. And contrary to most peoples' understanding, we do not need to have a completed software product before we think about testing.

As mentioned above, testing in practice can only really start around the coding stage.

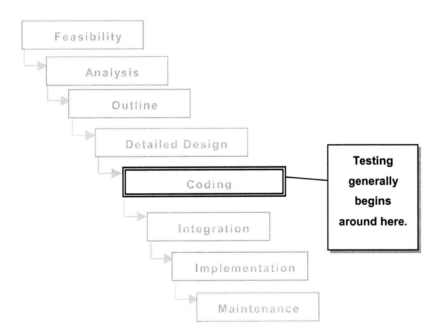

The Different Tester Titles Explained

It is at the coding stage that developers start to bring the ideas from the design phase to life. Programmers can then be assigned to work on the individual modules of code. In small projects one individual might be able to take care of developing a substantial portion of the program, whereas in more complex developments there may be an entire team of developers assigned to one component of the software being developed.

So, as in the diagram below, the entire application may be split into a number of separate units of code, allocated to individual programmers.

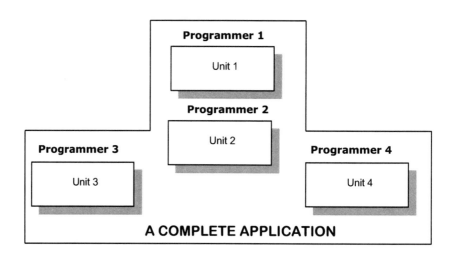

Unit Testing

Once each module or 'unit' of code is completed, the team or individual programmer must then test that module of code. This is the first stage of testing – and is known as **Unit Testing**.

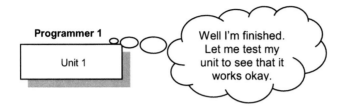

So we're out of the starting blocks (testing wise)!

Integration Testing

Now, once everybody's happy that their own individual units have been tested to perfection – we need to see how the individual units behave when they start *linking* to each other.

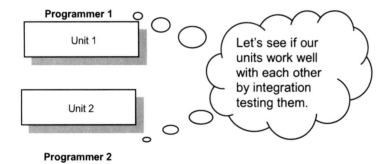

This form of testing, to check what happens when units of code are joined or *integrated,* is known as ... wait for it, **Integration Testing**.

Systems Testing

Once the individual units of code are working in harmony, the test teams will want to confirm that the entire software can operate as a well-balanced properly functioning, complete product. At this stage we might try it with dummy data and see how it responds as a whole. We might then venture further to see how it responds to the existing live systems which are currently being used by duplicating input data and running the new system in parallel and validating that it is indeed giving the desired results. This type of testing (which comes before the final User Acceptance Testing) is known as **systems testing**.

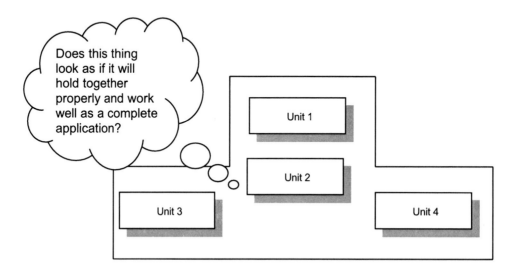

User Acceptance Testing

Now, after systems testing, the project is of course heading towards the final furlong of the development project. The software produced seems to be stable and robust as an entity in itself, and functioning well when implemented into a live environment. There still remains the issue of the user. Another specialist tester will need to come along and test the product on behalf of the user. This is known as User Acceptance Testing (or more commonly the **UAT** stage of testing) and is the stage at which the client or department receiving (or purchasing) the software product will satisfy themselves that this software does what it was supposed to do. UAT often involves testing the completed product in a far more rigorous way than the average user would.

UAT testing is the final stage before the client accepts the new system formally. Also see **black box** testing below.

Other Types of Testing

For the sake of completion I have listed below some other testing terms which I have frequently come across during my time in IT recruitment. Actually this is by no means an exhaustive list but I've listed these here simply because they will occasionally crop up on CVs and job specs too.

Alpha Testing

In-house testing of a completed software product. As soon as we are happy to release to external people to test alpha becomes ...

Beta Testing

Passing a software product to chosen external third-party users for purposes of testing.

Regression Testing

Ensuring that software is still working perfectly after someone has gone into it and made minor modifications and alterations to the way it works.

So What About Black Box and White Box Testing?

These are two terms you often hear bandied around by clients and candidates in this field. Black box testing is the catchall term for any type of testing that focuses on the *external* behaviour of the software. It's another term for testing that puts a focus on how the software behaves on the outside i.e. does it do what it's supposed to do? If not we can get the white box testers to look into why. White box testers are the ones who are far more interested in opening up the 'innards' of the software and tweaking the code in order to fix the problem.

User Acceptance testing is the perfect example of black box testing because it is purely concerned with making sure that the software does, for the user, what it says on the tin. With UAT we are concerned with how it *functions* and not what's happening in its internal *structure*. For this reason UAT is also known as **Functional testing**. From what we've just said you can also now appreciate that **White Box** testing is also commonly referred to as **Structural testing** too.

Tools Used in Testing

In the early days of programming, much of the testing was carried out manually, with (usually the programmer who wrote the code) scouring through the mass of code to find errors. Unsurprisingly, today much of this is automated through the use of testing tools. This is software which exists for the sole purpose of carrying out the laborious task of either finding errors in code, or simulating conditions that may stretch the program to failure.

Testing tools can be broadly categorised as being either:

Automated Test Tools

These are usually complete products available off-the-shelf to test programs during execution. **Mercury** is a good example of a vendor who provides automated test tools such as **WinRunner, LoadRunner** and **TestDirector**.

Manual Test Tools

These are generally products which allow testers to develop their own bespoke tools to test at various stages of development.

Interviewing Software Testers

Once again, this topic is so huge it could take up its own mini-guide. However I hope that, if there's one thing that has come across, it is that there are numerous different job titles within testing. The good news is that there are also just two big categories of tester; black box and white box. When you're interviewing a candidate, that's the first question you need to ask;

"Can you tell me where your key skills lie; towards *black* or *white box* testing?"

(You could of course substitute the key terms with *functional* or *structural*).

Also ask about their favourite test tools and specifically;

•   About their experience of using automated test tools and

•   Creating bespoke test scenarios using manual test tools.

Summary

I hope you can now see how testing is an IT world unto itself. There are hidden complexities and implications associated with each test role you recruit for. Overleaf is a Quick Glance Summary Sheet of the various different test phases and how they transpose onto the general development lifecycle.

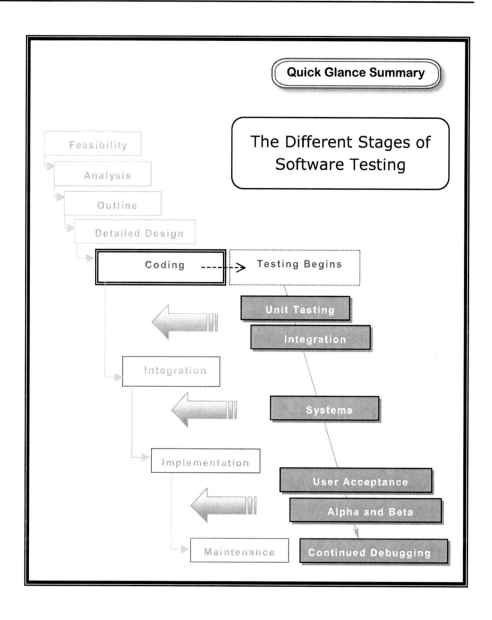

CHAPTER NINETEEN

Recruiting Database Developers

Introduction

In today's global economy, it's as valuable a commodity as gold, platinum or oil. It engulfs you while you're at work or at home. It is the seminal essence at the core of modern society, and in its many and varied forms, it cascades through the fibre and copper cables that make up the digital nervous systems of our cities. It zips around us surreptitiously day and night through the very air we breathe. As a society we are so completely hooked on **data**.

Data, Data Everywhere!

Should you feel the natural urge at this point to exclude yourself from the statement I've just made above, ask yourself the following. When was the last

GLASBERGEN

"We rarely back up our data. We'd rather not keep a permanent record of everything that goes wrong around here!"

time you opened up an email, purchased an item using a credit card, left a voicemail over a mobile phone network, shopped via the Internet, checked your online bank account, downloaded an mp3 song, followed the directions from a satellite navigation device, or added points to a supermarket loyalty card after shopping? All of these activities involved digital data transfer with the aid of highly intelligent storage systems somewhere along the way. The way in which you carried out many of the above activities will have been monitored, assessed and ultimately have yielded vital pointers as to who you are and your habits as an individual. Somewhere, in some form, disjointed and scattered, or complete and unified, your personality profile exists as an electronic demographic.

The problem for companies today lies not in *obtaining* the data they need. That particular skill has been honed to perfection by companies. In fact the last decade of the twentieth century has been dedicated to establish the best ways (covertly or otherwise) with which to extract data about customer behaviour (surveys, questionnaires, online forms, website monitoring software etc.) The problem arises not in obtaining data, but in making sense of the huge amounts of data flowing into a company's IT system. They are simply swamped with the stuff!

So, how does a commercial enterprise refine this colossal amount of raw *data* into coherent *information,* further into useful *knowledge* – and finally into invaluable *business intelligence*? This is where database technologies come in. Databases, data warehouses, storage area networks, OLAP, and data analysis tools allow the strategic leaders of a company to visualise that clear picture of who their customer is, and finally see the wood from the trees.

In this chapter I'll take you through many of the important database technologies of today, and outline the role of the database developer.

But first let's start with ...

Database Basics

What is a Database?

In computing terms, a database is application software which allows you to store data in a structured way. Undoubtedly, most of your clients today will be using a **Relational Database Management System (RDBMS)** in which to house their data. So RDBMS is the posh term for the common modern database and its associated suite of applications (I'll be using the two terms interchangeably from here on in). All modern RDMS applications allow us not only to record and store raw data, but also to systematically store the *relationships* between the data too. Far more interesting.

These sophisticated applications are even capable of yielding *data about data*, or **metadata**. They rely on a system of tables, which are automatically created within the application, and are perfectly arranged in a way that will enable the user to then query the data and build up that illusive clear picture.

A database can be **centralised** so that all of the data it holds and all of the applications of the RDBMS are looked after by one centralised processing computer; or the database could be **distributed** so that (although behaving as one large database) the data, the applications, and the processing are shared amongst a number of different computers often geographically detached.

The History of Databases

Before true RDBM systems, the first databases (though some now dispute whether we can even refer to these early applications as authentic 'databases') were those that followed a **flat file** or **flat model** approach. These systems simply recorded data in the most uncomplicated way possible. Generally, one line of plain text would be allocated to one complete record. The database would have no further functionality then that. In fact it offered no greater functionality or search capability than a piece of paper with the names and addresses of your favourite candidates scribbled on it, possibly in alphabetical order to make scanning easier, i.e.

> Adams, David. 49 Chester Avenue. London SW1. C++ Programmer.
>
> Aston, Susan. 21 The Drive. London EC10. Network Administrator.

As 'flat' as a piece of paper, this type of system was also occasionally referred to as being a **two-dimensional** database.

I think I'm probably right in saying that nobody uses these anymore (if however you do come across someone who does use one of these, let me know; the Science Museum in London would be very interested in speaking with them).

Next came databases which followed the **hierarchical model**. These systems allowed data to be stored in such a way that many-to-one relationships could be assigned. An example of this would be a record of one of your clients being linked to the records of certain candidates (those who work at that site). In the old days, with the earlier flat file systems, you would have had to scroll through the list of all of your candidates, and manually pick out those records which contained a reference to this employer. With hierarchical systems, searches could be made which allowed users to explore this **one-to-many** relationship easily.

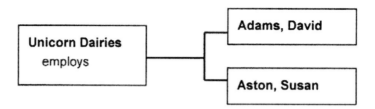

Again, this type of database is rarely used nowadays though some working examples still exist.

As inferred earlier, the database technologies which we should really focus on here are those linked to **relational databases (RDBMS)**. The idea was first formulated by Englishman, Edgar Codd whilst he was working at IBM in

1970. An acknowledged genius in this area, Codd also laid down the famous '**12 rules for Relational Databases**' (the gospel for RDBMS developers worldwide), and also coined the term **OLAP** (which we'll explain below).

Amongst the first databases which followed this model were **Ingres** (from Berkeley) and **System R** (from IBM), in around 1976. However the first commercial products, and the ones which would go on to have a lasting impact on the IT industry, were **Oracle** (from Oracle) and **DB2** (from IBM), which appeared in the early 1980s.

Relational databases are those which can link tables (like those from the flat file databases) in such a way that all of their complex, inter-relationships are also systematically recorded. Because of the multi-dimensional nature of the data recorded in a relation system, we can **query** it in very sophisticated ways. The manners in which this is done is thorough a querying language such as **SQL** (which we'll go into in a while); but this allows the user to bring back data groups which conform to a number of set criterion.

Let's summarise all of the above, with the help of an example.
Let's assume for a minute that you are a *time-travelling recruiter*. No, really!

This is how you would have instructed the computer to search for candidates using databases in each different era mentioned above:

The Flat file Search Era
"Show me my list of candidates!"
(That's it. The computer would show you candidates on record.)

The Hierarchical Search Era
"Find me all of our current candidates who have networking skills."

The Relational Search Era
"Find amongst my candidates, all those who can develop in Java, have over 5 years experience, require less than £50.00 per hour, can speak French, and are also available now."

Now that we've discussed how databases developed through history, let's make sure that you can 'speak the lingo' before we take a good look at some of the key products on the market today, and how to interview those database candidates.

Key Tools, Technologies and Concepts Associated with this Role

Over the next couple of pages are a few initial terms and concepts which you need to become familiar with before we can even attempt to discuss the intricacies of an Oracle database developer's mindset. These are the types of terms which frequently appear on CVs and job specs, but is really the precursor knowledge we need to have in place before we get into the nitty- gritty stuff. Think of this as *limbering up* for the juicier stuff to follow. Again, I'm just going to lay these out in a glossary format beginning with…

SQL and T-SQL

The way in which we carry out detailed searches, as mentioned in our time-travelling recruiter scenario earlier, is through the use of **Structured Querying Language (SQL)**. Developed by IBM, SQL is now the standard recognised querying language for most large databases. By a **querying** (alternatively known as **declaritive**) language we mean one which exists purely to query the data which is stored in an RDMS. SQL is not an **imperative** language (such as C++ or Java) in that it cannot be used to develop new application software from scratch. SQL is effectively a really efficient *runner* passing messages between the user and the database.

Through SQL you, the user, can issue instructions as to the type of data you wish to find (i.e. data which conforms to a number of set rules which you have defined in your query), and it will shoot off and come back with the results. So the statement

"Find me amongst my candidates, all those who can develop in Java, have over 5 years experience, require less than £50.00 per hour, can speak French, and are available now."

dictates five conditions which the SQL runner must satisfy when bringing data back from the database. In this way, SQL also creates new records, and deletes and updates existing records.

Database   **SQL**   **User**

Most of the large players in the database arena use SQL as their built-in querying tool. Similarly, most database developers (and database administrators) will have strong SQL skills, and will often be required to carry out SQL development. The big vendors have also played around with the SQL format and evolved their own variations to the language. So Microsoft's version is **Transact-SQL** (or **T-SQL**), which comes with their **MS SQL Server** database, and which developers in this product will prefer using. Oracle in fact has its own extension to SQL, which is known as **PL/SQL**.

Business Intelligence

Frustratingly, many of the terms in the area of data analysis sound as if they all pretty much mean the same thing. **Business Intelligence** can be thought of as an umbrella term for all of the strategies and ideas which come about once we spot the trends and relationships within the data we own. Most of the tools and concepts mentioned below are an intrinsic part of establishing sound business intelligence. The first of these is…

Data Warehouse

This is the term given to a very large and intelligent system which can collate data from a variety of sources (i.e. numerous databases). Additionally, most data warehouse systems are geared towards improving **business intelligence**, and supporting **Management Information Systems (MIS)** and **Decision Support Systems (DSS)**; see below for more on these. These often contain historical data or archived data held in a separate storage system to the **production database** (the live database that is being tapped into by the end-users on an on-going basis). In this way complex data warehouse processes (such as obtaining a snapshot of the current state of the global business operation for the purposes of a forthcoming board meeting) can be carried out without impeding on the capabilities of the live system. If the data warehouse's main function is to sub-categorised the data into business relevant groups (known as **data clustering**) for the purposes of analysis by say the marketing department or the accounts department, the resulting variation of a data warehouse is known as a **data mart**.

Data Mining

Formulating business intelligence strategies initially means drilling down into large masses of data (which may be housed in many separate databases or a data warehouse), and pulling out search results or sophisticated trends. This process is known as **data mining**. For this reason OLAP (see below) based tools and technologies are utilised.

OLAP

Online Analytical Processing (OLAP) is a term which is given to IT processes which allow the hidden, or subtle trends within data to be identified and analysed. This is a huge step up from just creating SQL queries. It takes searches to a new dimension (in fact another term for this type of search is a **multidimensional data model**), in that the patterns and relationships which were previously hidden can be isolated by viewing the data from many different perspectives. For this reason OLAP is one of the principal processes within the data mining process, and therefore in establishing business intelligence.

DSS

As the name implies, a **Decision Support System (DSS)** is any (usually IT-based) software which aids management when it comes to the arduous task of choosing which path to go down at critical points in the life of a business. They provide many of the answers to tricky 'what if' scenarios. Such systems are usually developed around the distinct needs of the business or industry sector (everything from medical diagnoses systems, to software that can help new home buyers come to a decision as to whether they are financially ready enough to make the move). When this sort of system is aimed at management it is often referred to as an **Executive Information System (EIS)** or **Management Information System (MIS)**.

Good. That's the limbering up out of the way. Now to tackle the meatier stuff. Let's go there now.

The Database Players

There are a number of players vying for dominance in this arena. IBM is an influential player simply because it has been in the race from the very beginning. Microsoft is in there simply because no influential software company should be without a database offering. However, **Oracle** is the technology which, for you, will continue to appear time and again on database CVs and job specs, and we will use this as a basis for studying database principles in this chapter.

Below are listed some of the key products on the market today.

Company	Product
Oracle	Oracle
IBM	DB2
Sybase	Sybase
Microsoft	SQL Server
MySQL	MySQL AB
Teradata	Teradata
UC Berkeley	Ingres

Note: As with many of the topics in this book, if I were to ever embark on writing 'The Complete Guide to Recruiting Database Specialists' it could potentially be just as substantial a work as the publication which you are currently reading. Each of the above databases has its own family of tools and technologies, and your candidates will list these on their CVs.

We're not going to explore all of these in this book; there are simply too many. What we'll do is study in detail the offerings from one big player in order to illustrate how all the rest work. So, for the remainder of this chapter I'm going to focus on **Oracle**, with a view to allowing you to see what other vendors also do with the tools at their disposal.

Without further ado, let me introduce you to …

The Oracle Corporation

Or Larry Almighty

There's an over-used joke in the IT industry which goes something like this.

> **Question:**
> *What's the difference between Larry Ellison and God?*
> **Answer:**
> *God doesn't think he's Larry Ellison.*

When most people think of Bill Gates, they instinctively conjure up an image of the archetypal techie; someone who might still become highly excited, even after having made his billions, at the very sight of a small, elegantly compiled piece of C++ code. Understated, and soft-spoken, one can still imagine Gates at home tapping away on a keyboard, in a small unassuming study in some secluded corner of his island retreat.

Not so, when one thinks of Larry Ellison. *The bad boy if IT,* his personal life is continuously in the glare of the IT paparazzi. Ellison is a much more colourful and flamboyant character, and he proffers plenty of material to them with which to work. He owns a fleet of aircraft (most of which he pilots himself whenever the mood strikes him). Another toy is the fourth largest yacht in the world (as well as the '**Sayonara**' which he sailed to victory in the Sydney to Hobart Yacht race in 1998). Home is an exclusive Japanese village styled complex in California; but in 2007 he reportedly bought in excess of $200million dollars worth of prime Malibu sea-front property. In many ways Ellison's life story is far more extraordinary than that of Gates, and it amazes me how this still hasn't been thrust into the face of a prominent Hollywood producer as a must-read screenplay. *Possibly the storyline would just be too much to swallow.*

Ellison stems from a humble working-class background; born out of wedlock to young nineteen-year-old girl who, months after his birth, handed him over to be raised by his Aunt in a Jewish neighbourhood in Chicago. It's fair to say that Ellison had tasted none of the silver-spoon trappings associated with the upbringing of his life-long archrival, William Gates III. And yet he has bounced erratically around the Forbes rich list, keeping industry analysts on their toes when predicting his next move; and at one stage even ousting Gates from top position of the richest man in the world. So that was Ellison the man; what about his work.

The Oracle Corporation

Ellison went on to form **Oracle Corporation** (named after its flagship product, the **Oracle RDBMS**). Since its inception in the late 1970s, he has retained the post of CEO in an organisation which proclaims itself to be the largest database company in the world. It should be mentioned here that IBM dispute this claim (citing their dominance over the mainframe market with their DB2 database system). However, it is widely acknowledged that Oracle is undoubtedly the second largest software company in the world, trounced only by Microsoft.

Oracle's Strategic Development

The product, which Oracle is famous for, is of course the **Oracle database** system itself. This was the first commercial database to make use of SQL (Structured Querying Language) to carry out it's querying of data. However Oracle (the company) has not exactly stood still as an organisation over the last two decades. It's no secret that they have always had one eye on becoming the biggest software company on the planet. Not only is Oracle a formidable corporate predator (having made acquisitions which included **PeopleSoft, Siebel, Hyperion** and **Agile Corporation** in just the three years prior to 2007), in the first few years of the 21st century it has also strengthened its strategic stance as a player in other software areas such as **Customer Relationship Management software (CRM)**, **Supply Chain Management (SCM)** and **Enterprise Resource Planning (ERP)** software.

The prolific rate of growth in the product range has never been an issue, but the naming convention of new products from Oracle has often caused confusion from the very beginning. And it continues to confuse new entrants to the database recruitment scene even today.

Not only are new products added to the range regularly (all with very similar sounding names), they are also upgraded regularly and re-classified according to some exotic (almost mystifying) version numbering system.

Interviewing Oracle Consultants

So what does an Oracle consultant actually do? This is the question I'm always asked on the courses. From my experience when training new recruiters, there are two areas which continue to cause a fair amount of confusion amongst all those involved in Oracle recruitment. The first of these is the naming and numbering convention of Oracle products. They all sound very similar.

The second area has to do with what an Oracle candidate actually does. On the latter point, the main thing to remember is that there is no single definition of an Oracle Consultant; so it will serve your best interest to get clients (those who insist on using this term) to explain in minute detail, their exact duties.

The Oracle Developer

The Oracle product range is huge and diverse; and so, by implication, the nature of Oracle roles must also mirror this diversity. Oracle developers can be core **database developers**; but they can also be **business process specialists, data warehouse specialists, forms consultants, ERP specialists**, or **CRM** experts (we'll explain these as we proceed).

The roles which I want to touch upon in this section are going to be those oriented towards the initial design and development of the database. The best way to ease ourselves into this area is by looking closely at the actual Oracle product range which your candidates will no doubt refer to in their CVs.

In other words, the best way to understand an Oracle developer is to look at the tools which they choose to highlight on their CV.

Let's look at some of the key products now, and hopefully it will all begin to make much more sense.

The Oracle Product Range

Below is a list of many of the key products that fall under the Oracle banner. I've separated these into simple bands, and have outlined how a candidate would use them. As I've mentioned earlier, the product names within Oracle are often similar sounding so you'll need to be aware of exactly which type of database technology (and therefore candidate) your client is really looking for. I've tried to make it as simple as possible by categorising them into digestible chunks and by assigning the main roles and technologies associated with each area; but it's best just to take a deep breath and dive in.

Oracle Databases

Product Name
Oracle Database 10g

Description
This is the flagship database software product as of December 2006. It comes in its own sub-flavours or 'editions'. Depending on the size of database which you need to create, or the features and functionality required, you could opt for **Standard, Enterprise, Express** or even **Personal** edition.

Role Titles Associated with This Area
Oracle Database Developer
Oracle Database Administrator

What We Should See On their CVs
Candidates who specialise on this product will have a CV dripping with core database terminology such as SQL, PL/SQL, Oracle SQL Developer, Oracle Forms, RAC, OLAP and many others (don't worry, these will become clearer as you read further into the chapter).

Oracle Applications

Product
Oracle E-Business Suite   Release 12 (Jan 2007)

Description
This product (also referred to as **Oracle Applications**) spearheads the Oracle attack on the **Enterprise Resource Planning** (ERP) market (see page 292). As the name implies it is a suite of applications which can be used to affectively implement ERP and CRM solutions. This is the suite in which you'll find distinct and separate product lines such as **Oracle Financials, Oracle HR, Oracle CRM** etc. However, within each of these product lines there is another layer of sub modules (each of which need to be licensed individually). Your candidates will often specialise in a particular product line as explained below.

Role Titles Associated with This Area
Oracle Applications Developer
Oracle E-business Suite Developer

What We Should See On their CVs
Although Oracle E-business suite (Oracle Applications) can sit on top of an Oracle database, **it doesn't necessarily follow that all Oracle E-business suite candidates are going to be database gurus**. Very often to the contrary, they will be far more knowledgeable about how to redesign the business processes in order to implement an affective ERP or CRM solution.

In fact an Oracle Financials consultant may spend a lot of their time explaining to you how they improved many areas of the financial function, or increased auditing transparency in their last role using modules (within Oracle Financials) such as **Oracle General Ledger** or **Oracle Treasury**. The list of modules, within each product line, within the E-business suite seems endless. Don't expect to become familiar with them all over-night, but don't be afraid to ask your candidates how the term on the CV fits into the business suite.

Oracle Platforms

Product
Oracle Application Server 10g

Description
You see what I mean about the naming conventions getting somewhat complicated. This product has nothing specifically to do with the Oracle Applications. It is in fact the Oracle version of a **platform**. However, this is a platform designed primarily for **grid computing**. Without going into grid computing in great detail, suffice it to say that this type of set-up is for IT operations which potentially might need to draw on huge processing capability. Grid computing allows parts of the business IT infrastructure to automatically draw on other (momentarily idle) parts of the IT system for extra processing power and support. Oracle Application Server 10g will enable grid computing capability on top of large (and sometimes disparate) IT system, and so this product (by its very nature) is also strongly linked to the **Oracle Fusion Middleware** product discussed below.

Role Titles Associated with This Area
Oracle Application Server Consultant
Oracle SAN/Data Storage Consultant

What We Should See On their CVs
Candidates specialising in Oracle Application Server 10g will generally be people who have had considerable experience in dealing with the *big stuff*. These include data storage solutions on a grand scale (I'd strongly recommend that you read the examples of grid computing which I've cited on page 49). We're referring here to servers which might utilise **SAN**s (**Storage Area Networks**), and data systems which are spread geographically across large areas (even globally), all acting as one intelligent data system. Consultants in this area may either be those who are more business oriented; and will have advised or helped design the initial solution. Or, they may be on the development side of the product; in which case they will have considerable expertise in designing databases but have now elevated their skills to a much larger scale, and would generally be using Oracle Fusion Middleware to allow it all to come together (see below).

Oracle Middleware Technologies

Product
Oracle Fusion Middleware

Description

In order to fully understand this product you'll need to have a sound understanding of the concept of **middleware**, so it is strongly recommended that you brush up on this by re-reading this topic on page 168. In fact rather confusingly, **Oracle Fusion Middleware** isn't a middleware in itself; it is a suite of Oracle tools (such as Oracle Application Server, JDeveloper, and Business Intelligence) and other middleware products which, when combined, allow a formidable middleware capability. Where there are company mergers or large-scale data integrations, this product would be at the working end in making sure that all of the disparate systems could link together and function.

Role Titles Associated with This Area

Oracle Database Developer

Oracle SAN/Data Storage Consultant

Oracle Data Warehouse Consultant

What We Should See On their CVs

Candidates using this Oracle product will invariably be those involved in systems integration or business integration. Many middleware products exist on the market today to help bring disparate IT systems together, but the use of the Oracle Fusion Middleware family implies that the resulting integration will need to deal with issues relating to business process, business intelligence as well as the orchestration of large amounts of data, and the interplay of content from a myriad of different business units.

For this reason consultants using this product will often make reference to **Service Oriented Architecture (SOA)** in their conversations with you. SOA is a term used to describe the underlying infrastructure which supports separate (yet linked) business process. So, for example, when you purchase an item online, there are a number of different business entities which get involved in the transaction (procurement, stock management, shipping etc.) SOA will be the underlying architecture which links all of these and allows data to be thrown around them without too much fuss.

SOAP (Simple Object Access Protocol) is a protocol which you'll often see used in conjunction with SOA. This is a protocol which uses web-type interfaces on all the different systems to enable them to unite and act as a unified SOA system.

ERP (Enterprise Resource Planning)

Is a software concept which enables better integration of a company's different business units and IT systems. Rather than designing a solution completely from scratch using, say, C++, ERP companies, such as SAP or Oracle, can be commissioned to use pre-made modules from their own library of software products to solve system integration and data compatibility problems across an enterprise. For this reason you will often hear of ERP consultants who specialise in vertical business modules such as SAP HR or Oracle Financials.

Oracle Development Tools

Product
Oracle Developer Suite

Description
Formally referred to as **Oracle Developer 2000**, this is the main suite of products used by those developing database systems from scratch with Oracle. This suite includes:

- **Oracle Designer**: A CASE tool (see page 193) for creating data models and business process models.

- **Oracle Forms**: This is a tool to very quickly create a fully functioning database from a library of pre-designed forms. Ideal for the simpler more urgent database requirements.

- **Oracle Reports:** This is a tool to design and generate reports from the stored data. The reports can be printed out or generated as web pages, excel spreadsheets or even PDF documents.

- **JDeveloper:** Oracle is a key promoter of the Java development environment; Jdeveloper allows developers to build the business logic (i.e. the thinking part or mathematical engine of the database) in a Java-oriented way.

Role Titles Associated with This Area
Oracle Database Developer
Oracle Database Administrator

What We Should See On their CVs
Candidates using products from the Oracle Developer Suite will be core database developers. This means that their primary concern will be to design and develop a functioning database in line with their client's needs. Candidates in this area will invariably be those involved in the conceptual design process (using Oracle Designer), the physical coding of the business logic or the bespoke design of forms for presenting data to the end user.

Summary

Phew! And so it goes on. There are numerous products from Oracle; all designed to develop, enhance or maintain database systems. And, the same can be said for most of the other major database vendors; such as Microsoft with their **SQL Server System**, and IBM with their **DB2** system.

Whichever database technology you are tasked with recruiting for (be it from Microsoft, IBM, Teradata etc.) do make sure that you spend some time in understanding the fundamentals first, and then become confident in the product range which the vendor is offering. If you're unsure it's worth asking the client or candidate to explain the specialisms, but at least now you'll (hopefully) understand the explanations they come back with.

CHAPTER TWENTY

Recruiting Administration and Support Roles

Introduction

You've probably never noticed. You were either too busy scurrying off to make a cup of tea when they came, or just too eager to see your computer come back to life again, so that you could continue updating your Facebook profile. But there is something so special about this group of people. This chapter is dedicated to all of those unsung heroes of IT who quietly emerge from the background when things go wrong and who keep our IT systems up and running. To those unfortunate soles who have to patiently listen to our inane mumblings as we attempt to explain what we did to finally destroy our desktop PC once and for all.

<table>
<tr><td colspan="2">STRAIGHT TO</td></tr>
<tr><td>➤</td><td>IT Administration roles
Page 296</td></tr>
<tr><td>➤</td><td>Networking primer
Page 299</td></tr>
<tr><td>➤</td><td>Helpdesk roles
Page 305</td></tr>
<tr><td>➤</td><td>Summary sheet
Page 305</td></tr>
</table>

"You have to solve this problem by yourself. You can't call tech support."

It's worth paying special attention to their mannerisms as they start to diagnose the problems in your system. You'll eventually realise that the 21st century IT support person has developed an incredibly measured, detached yet pleasant bedside manner when it comes to diagnosing their patients' ailments (either remotely on the phone or when pottering around underneath your desk). These mannerisms, I've concluded, have evolved after decades of dealing with an abusive and impatient client base who has never given IT support services the recognition they truly deserve. As a result this group of people has learned to efficiently locate the source of the problem, solve it quickly and disappear, fast. They're not allowed the luxury of the disapproving *tutt-tutting* which we so readily put up with from the mechanic servicing our beloved family car. They have learned over the years that, no matter how irate the person, their best chances of success is to calmly and systematically work through the various options, and move on to the next case. And so they set to work, one by one peeling away layer after layer of the IT architecture. You try to keep up, but very soon they leave you behind and are so deep within the system that they are now communing with the very 'soul' of the beast. Just a dark blue command line interface; where they start to tweak the registry, or adjust the BIOS settings. And eventually managing to breath miraculous life back into the system. Let's pay homage then to the IT support, administration and data-back up people, starting with …

IT Administration Roles

Whenever you see the title of 'administrator' being applied to a role it, by and large, means '**responsible for the maintenance and upkeep of the X**'. Where 'X' generally denotes a network, a web site, an entire IT architecture or a database. So the key roles which you will be asked to source in this area are

*   Network Administrator
*   Website Administrator
*   Systems Administrator
*   Database Administrator

Once again, this topic is so vast that I could probably set off and compile another complete book based around the various attributes, tools and skills of the above roles; but for now we'll keep it simple.

Administrators of any IT system (i.e. the database, network, or website) really have three key concerns

1.   To ensure that their system is currently running smoothly,

2.   To have plans and strategies in place to make sure the system *continues* to run smoothly as conditions change, and

3.   To have plans and strategies in place in order to cope when the very worst eventuality occurs.

The Duties of a Network / Database Administrator

In many ways the duties of these two administrators are similar, and so I have outlined these collectively. These include:

*   Ensuring that the layout of the network/database is robust and stable enough to cater for current user demand. This will initially have been a key responsibility of the network architect or database developer when designing the original system. Thereafter it is the administrator who will need to be comfortable with when it comes to tweaking and adjusting on an ongoing basis. This is the reason why network administrators always keep themselves up to speed with regards existing trends in hardware and operating systems; and also why the best database administrators (DBA) aren't afraid to tweak or even re-develop elements of their database (including re-programming SQL based elements within the database).

*   Setting up user accounts with usernames, passwords, and assign appropriate clearance levels.

• Troubleshooting day-to-day user issues. This includes carrying out diagnosis on which of these problems are simply blips in an otherwise smooth operation, and which are pointers towards deeper-rooted inadequacies within the network or database.

• Ensuring that the network or database is set up in a scalable format, so that it will accommodate future growth. For networks this means handling an ever-increasing range of voice and data traffic. This is known as **capacity planning**.

• Implementing tools and techniques to prevent intrusion, and designing strategies to guard against ongoing internal and external security threats.

• Continually carrying out **performance tuning** of the network or the database, so that as traffic grows the entire system is always operating at an optimum level.

• As far as database administrators are concerned, there also needs to be a regular focus on the cleansing of data. So they carry out the scheduled restructuring of the database so as to optimise it's performance. This is known as **data cleansing** and **defragmentation**.

A Quick Primer on Network Terminology

Or *If you CAN, just PAN, MAN!*

Networking CVs can often be amongst the most mind-numbingly long-winded documents you'll come across in IT recruitment. Candidates will take great pride in waxing lyrical about the various networks which they have either designed or implemented during their careers. These CVs are right up there in a league of their own when it comes to spewing out TLAs (Three Letter Acronyms) and complex IT jargon. During interviews you'll find yourself fending off deep slumber as the candidate explains how amusing it is

"… that even today Ethernet protocol and Token Ring, after all these years, still came out head and shoulders above the 100Base T and newer IEEE 802.11 technologies protocol when trying to trying to link LANs together across a CAN."

But be in no doubt. These people are a valuable commodity in IT. Networking may not be as sexy as Java or C#, but sexy technologies will rise and wane with the economic climate. However your clients will always, always need a secure and robust IT network. Every large corporation will, at its core, rely on a sound, stable network architecture whether in a times of recession or boom. And for this reason IT recruiters sourcing network specialists are always kept busy.

The good thing here is that for all the verbosity of the terminology associated with this area, most of the jargon connected to networking will fall into one of the following simple categories:

The scale of network

You'll often find networking candidates referring to computer networks in terms of the geographical area covered. Generally a network which is restricted to a single building or site is referred to as a **Local Area Network** (or **LAN**), though its not always correct to think of these as being small networks. If such networks expand outwards to a group of interconnected buildings such as in a sprawling hospital or university complex (though still not needing an external third party such as BT to make the connection between buildings) this situation is often coined a **Campus Area Network** (or **CAN**). A network becomes a **Wide Area Network** (or **WAN**) once it spans a much larger geographical area, and strictly speaking, when it has the need of a third party telecoms player to make the connection (i.e. to make use of telephone lines or fibre optic cables to allow LANs in two different cities to be connect). So if your company has offices around the world over which you send internal emails to your colleagues, then it is the WAN part which is allowing the two LANs to communicate across the Atlantic Ocean. In fact, loosely speaking, the Internet can be thought of as a large public WAN. Another term which can be pulled into this category is one used for a citywide network, usually referred to as a **Metropolitan Area Network** (or **MAN**). So a MAN may incorporate a number of LANs and CANs in its infrastructure. As we surge into the 21st century the terms continue to evolve and we will hear variations on all of the above themes such as **WLAN** (Wireless LAN) and even **PAN** (Personal Area Networks which have a radius of just one metre around an individual, and are emitted by devices such as PDAs).

Topologies

The configuration, or way of laying out the components of a network (i.e. will the computers be linked in a straight line, or in circle etc.), is often referred to as the topology of the network. Some common ones are **bus**, **star** and **ring**.

Protocols

One of the most fascinating aspects of network design (no really!) is how architects set up intricate rules of communication between computers on a network. This implies that there are actually a myriad of different ways in which data could potentially travel around the network. It's ultimately up to the resident network guru to implement the most efficient and cost-effective set of rules for their circumstances. These sophisticated *rules* to establish communication between devices on a network are known as the **protocols**. Common examples of protocols seen on CVs and job specs are **Ethernet**, **Token Ring** and **Frame Relay**.

So that was a quick primer on networking, but let's continue with the support and administration roles which you'll come across, starting with a story of …

Extreme Disaster Recovery

Or *Superheroes Can't Play Pool*

As Sid stepped into the business class cabin of the aircraft, all eyes seemed to immediately become trained on him. Not that there was anything unique about Sid's appearance. Far from it. And being his closest mate for over twenty years, I felt it my duty to remind him of that from time to time. Joking aside however, in reality Sid was more like a brother to me than a friend.

In fact Sid, Imi (he of the project manager wife fame in Chapter 10) and I had been inseparable for nearly three decades. Even now at the age of forty, and with the advent of our own wives and kids, it still often felt to me as if the guys were turning up on my doorstep on Friday evenings to ask my wife if I could come and 'kick a ball around until tea-time'. As was expected amongst us guys, we had spent the last twenty odd years ribbing each other about every possible thing. Sid would relish in taunting my 'clearly misunderstood' fashion sense since the age of twelve. I in turn mocked everything about him; from the dubious arrangement of his facial hair, to his lack of prowess when it came to using a pool cue.

But when we left Sid at terminal three of Heathrow airport that day, Imi and I were both secretly anxious. Very anxious.

For even though Sid was born in Hackney, and had never really travelled much further out of the UK than on a school trip to the Calais, his non-European features today took on a significance which we couldn't ever have foreseen. Not even in our wildest dreams. For Sid's real name was Sayeed Khan. And although his father came from India, Sid had acquired much of his facial characteristics from his Afghani mother. To the uninitiated, Sid had a distinctly Middle Eastern appearance. And that summer, in that particular September month, those Middle Eastern features had taken on bizarrely unexpected connotations.

Seven days earlier, a bunch of young Arab men had tried to prove some sort of point by flying two airliners into the World Trade Centre in New York, wiping out some 2000 innocent lives in the process. Since then none of us quite knew what to make of the world we now lived in. Suddenly everything had changed. Suddenly these were precarious times.

"It was ridiculous," Sid said.

"All the passengers were staring at me. They were evidently distraught the minute I boarded the plane!" Sid exclaimed as he regaled the whole story for us back at the snooker club.

"As I went to take my seat, the woman sitting next to me actually had beads of sweat forming on her brow. In fact I think she was actually scanning me for unsightly bulges in my jacket!"

At that moment I was going to throw in a "*Sayeed*, we've been warning you about your unsightly bulges for years!" but, after a stern look from Imi, decided against it.

"So, how the hell did you calm the situation?" we asked.

"Simple," shrugged Sid. "As the plane started to taxi towards the runway, I called over an air hostess loud enough so that everybody could hear, and in my strongest cockney accent, ordered two glasses of red wine, a ham sandwich and packet of pork scratchings!"

Sid told us that the ensuing sigh of relief which reverberated around the cabin, was loud enough to drown out the noise of take off!

"To relieve the tension, I'd have ordered a Las Vegas call girl, and a copy of Washington's inaugural speech had they been on the menu!" Laughed Sid.

Of course his fellow passengers weren't to blame. They couldn't have known two important points about our friend. Firstly, that Sid didn't really harbour any religious convictions at all. In fact Sid had pretty much abandoned spirituality completely around his sixteenth birthday, on the day that two of the trustees of the local mosque had chased us down Hackney Marshes yielding baseball bats.

This was following young Sid's (alleged) advances towards their niece at summer school, the fragrant and ever-popular Nabeela. Since that particular episode Sid had never been seen near a religious establishment, Muslim, Jewish, Mormon or otherwise.

Secondly, and more importantly, the other passengers could not have known that Sid had, over the years, become an extremely accomplished IT consultant who was now working for one of the world's leading disaster recovery companies.

In fact on that particular September day, as people were pouring out of a shattered New York, Sid was *flying in*. He was one of the select group of individuals who was actually going to walk into the devastation, *and try to make it all better again*. His client on this occasion was an investment bank based in Manhattan, and in around eight hours Sid would be dropped into the carnage, into the very eye of the storm, to help them piece together the biggest disaster recovery project that the planet had ever seen.

"You should have seen the destruction," whispered Sid shaking his head. "Just twisted metal and rubble. Armageddon."

"How did you ever set about … I mean where do you start?" I stuttered in open admiration.

"Well just to make matters worse, when we got there, we realised that the collapse of the towers had actually knocked out the client's back-up site a couple of miles down the road."

"You're joking. What the hell did you do then?"

As was his way in such situations, Sid slipped into an irritatingly 'matter-of-fact' tone and continued, as if calmly relaying instructions on how to install a new mouse.

"Fairly straight forward really. We couldn't use the existing site. So we had to build another one!"

"What!" We stared at him in disbelief.

"Well, *not from ground up.* That would be ridiculous. But we set about the next best thing. We secured one of the large New York hotels and cleared the rooms of all existing guests (which wasn't difficult under the circumstances). After that we simply had to take over all of the floors, install an enterprise level client-server network, bring in a bunch of Cisco routers, hard wire an IBM blade server network, renegotiate SLA's with the Reuters and Bloomberg market feed guys to supply the hotel, set up secure wireless network domains for all the two hundred users behind a fairly solid firewall, assign usernames and passwords and restore the accounts database from the UK back up. After that it was fairly standard stuff. Brought in the administration teams and the traders were pretty much up and ready to play!"

Imi and I looked at each other and then stared at Sid with a sense of complete wonder. Speechless. This was our friend, and we were both so proud that he had come such a long way. Following a few minutes of silent admiration and contemplation, I looked up at Sayeed, and said the only thing I could to truly sum up the love we felt for him at that moment.

"Yeah pug face, but you're still crap at pool."

Imi sprayed out his coke, and a disgusted Sid got up and marched over to the pool table once more. Slamming a pound coin onto the table he grabbed a cue and stared back at me. This time with a determined fire in his eyes.

Like he stood a snowball's chance.

Helpdesk Summary: 1st, 2nd and 3rd Line Support

I am asked to clarify these roles time and again during the training courses. And it's hardly surprising really. During my career I have seen so many variations to these job titles. What may be considered to be 'First line support' by one of your clients, might well be deemed 'second line support' by another, and even 'Call logger' by another. But you need to be clear in your own mind as to how you're going to classify the various helpdesk candidates who turn up for interview. Here's a good firm starting point when setting about the definitions of these roles:

Call Logger

This is a non-technical person who exists primarily to verbally pacify the irate caller, enough at least to be able to extract clear indications as to the broad nature of their problem. Either they will issue a ticket number at this stage, or pass the caller on to someone who may be able to swiftly solve the problem. They will escalate the call to

First Line Support

This is the first line of phone-based technical expertise which exists either to solve the most simple of problems (of course what I mean by 'simple' here is still a technical expertise level somewhat higher than the lay IT DIYer at home). Therefore technical issues relating to desktop problems, and peripherals are handled at this level. These include the usual suspects such as "Why can't I print today", "My mouse isn't working", or "Where has the e-mail icon gone from my desktop." These people can generally guide you to safer ground on the phone by expertly talking you through a number of mouse clicks and asking you to re-boot an inordinate number of times. However, if it isn't solvable here, they will escalate your call to

Second Line Support

These are technically more experienced than 1st line support, and are able to crack the more tricky technical knots which you have managed to tie yourself into. Still phone-based (though some of your clients may vary from this definition), the problems dealt with here relate to deeper networking and operating system issues. This may well involve looking into the server, or database. These people will generally have no faith in your driving capabilities at all and will remotely take charge of your mouse and your computer without a by-your-leave. If you've not experienced this yet, trust me, there is no greater feeling of inadequacy than that of a user who's PC has suddenly been taken over by an expert remote user. And worse, the machine, slow and cumbersome in your hands, now seems to be dancing a sublime and effortless Waltz with its new partner, as if lifted to levels of previously inexperienced ecstasy by a far more proficient practitioner. Of course if the problem still can't be solved at this level, you've really messed up. Put down the mouse, step away from the desk and await

Third line Support

By most definitions this is as high as it gets in support and is not strictly phone-base support (though I have now heard of corporations using the term fourth line support they've never really explained it to me in anywhere near a convincing manner). Re-engineering the server or re-designing the entire network is primarily the level at which these people operate. Highly qualified, and with the relevant accreditations, these will be IT specialiasts who in their next role are looking to make the move into becoming full-blown Network Engineers and Technical Architects. If they can't solve it, send the machine back to the manufacturer!

CHAPTER TWENTY-ONE

And Finally...

So there it was, my attempt to encapsulate the world of IT recruitment within a few chapters of a book. I hope this publication has gone some way to helping you better understand the IT landscape in which you operate. I am sure you'll agree that the individuals who work in this arena form the very backbone of business operations around the world. Their creations will continue to explode into the public domain and impact us at work and at home. The hardware they create is working in unfathomably more efficient ways, and the applications they create continue to astound us day by day. You as a recruiter in the IT industry are responsible for sourcing the very lifeblood of businesses in the 21st century. It just remains for me to say a big thank you for allowing me to lead you through this journey into the world of IT and the IT department.

Your Feedback

I welcome your views on this book. I look forward to hearing from you if you have positive feedback which we can share with others on the book's website, and also any ideas on how we might improve future editions. Email me directly at **ayub@holistica.co.uk**.

Further Resources

It is of course impossible for a book like this to include every single acronym relating to each new technology that appears, especially since IT itself moves so rapidly. So this is also the stage at which I offer you some additional pointers as to how you might keep abreast of developments in your industry. Of course the last few pages of The Guide are dedicated to some shameless self-promotion and point you towards Holistica's own training products, but before that I have listed below a few additional resources which may help you on an ongoing basis.

Internet based

www.holistica.co.uk/glossaryforrecruiters.html

My own company's free downloadable glossary for those in IT recruitment. Help yourself!

www.wikipedia.org

The leading player in the world of online encyclopaedias. Excellent as a first stop for understanding any IT acronym or jargon. My only word of warning would be to cross-reference anything you acquire from here with another different source to ensure veracity.

www.webopedia.com

Similar to Wikipedia but in my view much better for technology in business.

www.whatis.com

In my view the most thorough and definitive collection of IT terms on the net. This is however a very technical site and oriented towards actual IT practitioners.

www.google.com   or   www.ask.com

Just Google it! Or of course use any search engine to see how they explain the IT term you're confused about.

Hard Copy Journals

Computer Weekly (Available as print or digital)
You are now at the stage at which you should be able to pick up journals like this and understand what the movers and shakers in the industry are up to.

Computing (Available as print or digital)
Once again an excellent resource to keep you up to speed on new technologies and industry movements.

Index

Holistica's Training Courses
for People in IT Recruitment

The promotional bit

As you are now doubt aware this book would not have been written were it not for those within the IT recruitment industry coming to Holistica's training events, enjoying the learning experience and pushing my colleagues and me to spread the word further with projects like this. So if you're totally new to the industry, or a seasoned recruiter in need of a refresher, or a department manager who thinks this could be beneficial; why not meet us in person and experience our live instructor-led workshops for yourself. We would be delighted to see you at one of our events. Our range of courses are highlighted below and cover everything from the basics to the more complex vertical areas of IT and telecoms recruitment.

- The Recruiter's Guide to IT Fundamentals
- The Recruiter's Guide to IT Roles
- The IT Recruitment Masterclass
- The Recruiter's Guide to Emerging IT Concepts
- Recruiting Software Developers with Java, C# and .NE
- Recruiting SAP and ERP Specialists
- Recruiting Software Testers
- Recruiting in the Telecoms and 3G arena
- Internet Recruitment Masterclass

Visit our website at **www.holistica.co.uk** for detailed course outlines, dates and costs etc. To see our client list and delegate feedback visit **www.holistica.co.uk/ clientreviews.html**.

If you have any further questions you can always email us at **info@holistica.co.uk**.

I hope we get a chance to meet at some point in the future.

In the meantime I wish you health, happiness and success in whatever you do.

Ayub Shaikh

CPSIA information can be obtained at www.ICGtesting.com
Printed in the USA
LVOW112345230812

295745LV00005B/253/P